PostgreSQL for DBA

Volume 1 Structure and administration

Federico Campoli

First edition, January 2019

Copyright

Preface

This is the first volume of a book series which covers PostgreSQL from the database administrator's point of view. The reason why I decided to write it is because the DBA have specific needs that are not covered in other books or are described with different order or depth.

A DBA is a strange combination of theory and practice. Because of a mix of strictness and loose rules it's quite difficult to explain what exactly a DBA does. Working with databases requires passion and knowledge mixed with empathy and pragmatism, which helps to understand what the DBMS is thinking. With commercial products knowledge is commonly limited by the vendor's documentation and missing parts are filled by the DBA's personal experience. Working with a free DBMS like PostgreSQL the source code's availability facilitates the knowledge acquisition. The PostgreSQL's codebase is superb poetry written in C. Just reading the comments builds an intimate relation between the cold binary programs and the geniuses contributing to the PostgreSQL project.

A day in the life of a DBA does not have fixed boundaries. The "day" can be just one day or spawn over several months, if for example there are long procedures to be executed inside well controlled maintenance windows. Each new day is different from the previous with a combination of various duties. Those are daily tasks, monitoring, proactive thinking and emergency handling.

Daily tasks

Under the group of daily tasks there are all procedures which are well consolidated on the documents and in the DBA mind. For example, configuring the PostgreSQL's memory parameters should be something immediate which does not require reading documentation. Any task in this category is successful if it remains completely unnoticed. It is not unlikely for the production environment that routine tasks are performed in antisocial hours like Sunday night or early hours of working day.

Monitoring

A system without monitoring is a one way ticket to the disaster. Whatever solution is used it should be something simple to configure and with a decent low rate of false positives. Having a nagging monitoring is exactly the same as not having one at all where important alerts will be lost in the background noise.

Proactive thinking

Proactive thinking is the distinctive mark between a good DBA and a cheap professional. The capability of building a mental map for finding root cause and solution for any possible issue, projected in the near future, can make the difference between spending night sleeping and working frantically before next day begins. Reacting to the issues is fine. Trying to prevent them is much better. Proactive handling of tasks is strictly related with monitoring.

Emergency handling

S*** happens, it's a life fact. Sooner or later a disaster will strike requiring maximum effort from the database experts to recover systems. It doesn't matter if the issue is caused by an user screwing up a database table, an hardware failure or a fleet of Vogon spaceships coming to demolish the earth. The rule Number Zero when in an emergency is *never guess*. Guessing without knowledge can lead to the database destruction.

Failure is not an option

The failure is not an option. Despite this statement is quite pretentious it is also the mandatory attitude for being a decent DBA. Task failure is not acceptable. The database is the core of any application and therefore is the most important element of the infrastructure.

In order to achieve this impossible level of service the correct mental attitude is that any task is single shot. Everything must run perfectly on the first run like not having a rollback plan. However the rollback procedure must be prepared and tested alongside with the main task in order to get a smooth restore of the previous state if required. It's also very important to have a checklist and remembering each step. Having a checklist document is good but this does not mean that the DBA should rely only on the document. Remembering the checklist's steps allows the DBA to catch the exact point of any possible failure ensuring a rapid fix when it happens.

RTFM

The acronym RTFM stands for Read The F*****g Manual. It's quite obvious that reading the manual is the perfect approach for finding correct information or at least a hint for finding the solution.

The false confidence or a lack of humbleness make people to forget how important it is to read documentation. Understanding documentation is the next step, and it is far from simple indeed. Especially if DBA background is poor or the reader have preconceptions which alters the word meanings.
My hope is that reading this book will give you a good starting point for administering PostgreSQL.

Special thanks

I can't say thank enough to Laura Gaigala for the priceless help in reviewing the book.

Intended audience

Database administrators, System administrators, Developers

Book structure

This book assumes the reader knows how to perform basic user operations such as connecting to the database and creating tables.

The book covers the basic aspects of database administration from installation to cluster management.

A couple of chapters are dedicated to the logical and physical structure in order to show two sides of the same coin. Then the maintenance along with the backup and restore completes the the picture. This is not exhaustive but is good enough to start getting "hands on" with the database. There is also chapter dedicated to the developers giving advice that can seem quite obvious.

Text conventions

Within the book there are different styles which have specific meanings.

COMMAND

Text enclosed in this frame is a list of operating system commands. It should be possible to copy paste without modification and have it run on the OS.

QUOTE

Text enclosed in this frame is quoted from the from documentation or help output. When appropriate there are references pointing to the original document.

ATTENTION

Text enclosed in this frame lists things to pay particular attention.

EXAMPLE

Text enclosed in this frame are examples.

Version and platform

This book is based on PostgreSQL version 11 compiled from source and running on Slackware GNU Linux 14.2.
The install procedure from the packages covers both debian and rpm based distributions.
For deb the operating system used is Devuan GNU Linux 2.0
for the rpm the operating system is CentOS 7.

All shells are written in bash.

Contents

Part I

Introduction

Chapter 1

PostgreSQL at a glance

PostgreSQL is a first class product coming with enterprise class features. This chapter will walk trough the features available with the version 11. But first things first, we'll check how everything started.

1.1 A long time ago, in a galaxy far, far away...

Picking up the work of Berkeley's Professor Michael Stonebraker, Marc G. Fournier in 1996 asked if there were any volunteers interested in contributing to the Postgres 95 project.

QUOTE

```
Date: Mon, 08 Jul 1996 22:12:19-0400 (EDT)
From: "Marc G. Fournier" <scrappy@ki.net>
Subject: [PG95]: Developers interested in improving PG95?
To: Postgres 95 Users <postgres95@oozoo.vnet.net>
Hi... A while back, there was talk of a TODO list and development
    moving forward on Postgres95 ...
at which point in time I volunteered to put up a cvs archive and
    sup server so that
making updates (and getting at the "newest source code") was
```

Some people replied to Mark's email. Bruce Momjian,Thomas Lockhart, and Vadim Mikheev, started working on the project.

Today, after more than 20 years, PostgreSQL is a robust, reliable, enterprise class relational database.

1.2 Features

Each time a new major version is released it adds a set of new features to PostgreSQL. What follows is a small excerpt of the capabilities of the latest version of PostgreSQL.

1.2.1 ACID compliant

The word ACID is an acronym for Atomicity, Consistency, Isolation and Durability. An ACID compliant database ensures those rules are enforced at all times.

- The atomicity is enforced when a transaction is "all or nothing". For example: If a transaction inserts a group of new rows and just one row violates the primary key then the entire transaction must be rolled back leaving the table as if nothing happened.

- The consistency ensures the database is constantly in a valid state. The database steps from one valid state to another valid state with no exceptions.

4

- The isolation is enforced when the database status can be reached as if all the concurrent transactions were run in serial.

- The durability ensures the committed transactions are saved on durable storage. In the event of a database crash the database must restore itself to the last valid state.

1.2.2 MVCC

PostgreSQL ensures atomicity, consistency and isolation via the MVCC. The acronym stands for Multi Version Concurrency Control. The mechanism is incredibly efficient, it offers great level of concurrency while keeping the transactions snapshots isolated and consistent. However there is a single disadvantage in its implementation. We'll see in a detail in 7.6 how MVCC works and the reason why there's no such thing as an update in PostgreSQL.

1.2.3 Write ahead logging

The durability is implemented in PostgreSQL using the write ahead log (WAL). In short, when a data page is updated in the volatile memory the change is saved immediately to a durable location - the write ahead log. The page is written to the corresponding data file later. In the event of the database crash the write ahead log is scanned and all the inconsistent pages are replayed on the data files. Each segment size by default is 16 MB and automatically managed by PostgreSQL. The write happens in sequence from the segment's start to the end. When it's full PostgreSQL switches to a new one with log switch.

1.2.4 Point in time recovery

When PostgreSQL switches to a new WAL this could be a new segment or a recycled one. If the old WAL is archived in a safe location it's possible to get a copy of the physical data files while the database is running. The hot copy, alongside with the archived WAL segments have all the necessary information and sufficient to recover the database to the consistent state. The recovery by default terminates when all archived data files have been replayed. It's possible to stop the recovery at any given point in time.

1.2.5 Standby server and high availability

Standby server is a database configured to stay in continuous recovery. This way a new archived WAL file is replayed as soon as it becomes available. This feature was first introduced in PostgreSQL 8.4 as warm standby. Starting from version 9.0 PostgreSQL can be configured also as a hot standby which allows connections for read only queries.

1.2.6 Streaming replication

The WAL archiving doesn't work in real time. The segment is shipped only after a log switch and in a low activity server this can leave standby database behind master for a while. It's possible to limit the problem using the archive_timeout parameter which forces a log switch after given number of seconds. However, using streaming replication a standby server can get the wal blocks over a database connection in almost real time. This feature allows transmission of physical blocks over a conventional database connection.

1.2.7 Logical replica

Since version 9.4 PostgreSQL supports logical decoding of wal changes. Since then, third party tools have been developed to take advantage of logical decoding. Starting with version 10 PostgreSQL added a set of SQL commands for configuring native logical replica.

1.2.8 Procedural languages

PostgreSQL has many procedural languages. The most popular is indeed pl/pgsql. However it's possible to write a procedure in many other development languages like pl/perl and pl/python. Anonymous function blocks are also supported using the DO keyword.

1.2.9 Procedures and functions

PostgreSQL supports function execution with a simple SELECT on a function which runs in a single transaction. Therefore functions do not allow transaction management within the function's body.

Since version 11 PostgreSQL supports procedures which are executed using CALL statement and allow to commit or rollback transactions blocks within the procedure's body.

1.2.10   Partitioning

Since version 10 PostgreSQL supports declarative partitioning.

Version 11 supports both global indices/primary keys and foreign keys pointing a partitioned table.
Version 11 has an option to create a new default partition, for data which doesn't fall into any of defined partitions range or list.
Eows that change their partitioning criteria are moved across the partitions automatically.

1.2.11   Cost based optimizer

The cost based optimizer, or CBO, is one of the PostgreSQL's points of strength. The execution plan is dynamically determined from data distribution and from query parameters. PostgreSQL also supports genetic query optimizer GEQO and, from the version 11 queries can be planned using the JIT compiler.

1.2.12   Multi platform support

PostgreSQL runs on almost any unix flavor and Microsoft Windows.

1.2.13   Tablespaces

Tablespace support allows to have a fine grained distribution of the data files across file systems. In chapters 5.10 and 7.5 we'll see how to take advantage of this powerful feature.

1.2.14   Views

The read only views have been part part of PostgreSQL since early releases. Recently has been added support for materialized views and updatable views.

1.2.15 Triggers

Triggers are well supported on tables and views. There is also an implementation of event triggers. Triggers can be used to configure and implement updatable views in complex view definitions.

1.2.16 Constraint enforcement

PostgreSQL supports primary keys and unique keys to enforce a table's data integrity. The referential integrity is possible with the foreign keys. We'll take a look to the data integrity in 6

1.2.17 Extension system

PostgreSQL implements a very efficient extension system. The command CREATE EXTENSION allows installation of new features with ease.

1.2.18 Federated tables

PostgreSQL supports federated tables. This is a SQL/MED implementation that allows to point foreign tables to heterogeneous external data sources. Some foreign data wrappers also support write mode.

1.2.19 RLS

Row level security allows to define security policies on a table in order to filter rows on specific criterias. The most common use is to have rows filtered per database user in order to restrict data access to the personal data only.

1.2.20 ALTER SYSTEM

This feature gives the DBA the power to alter some of configuration parameters directly from the SQL client. The parameters are validated when the command is sent to the database. Invalid values are spotted immediately reducing the risk of having an hosed cluster because of syntax errors.

Chapter 2

Database installation

In this chapter we will see how to install PostgreSQL on Devuan Gnu Linux. We'll first see how to compile PostgreSQL from source and then how to use the packages shipped via the pgdg apt repository.

There are advantages and disadvantages to both procedures. Compiling from source offers fine grained control of all aspects of the configuration of the binaries. It also doesn't have the risks of unwanted restarts when upgrading and it's possible to install and upgrade the binaries without administrator privileges.

The packaged install is easier to manage when deploying new binaries to a server, in particular if there is a large number of installations to manage. The binary packages are released shortly after a new release is done.

2.1 Install from source

When using configure script with the default settings the install requires root access. That's because the permissions of the target location /usr/local doesn't allow writes to normal users. The following method uses a different install location and requires root access only for creating the operating system user which will manage the postgres process and will own the data area. On certain distributions it will be necessary to add some dependency packages in order to compile PostgreSQL.

It's also a good idea to have a dedicated user for running the PostgreSQL process.

COMMAND

```
useradd -d /home/postgres -s /bin/bash -m -U postgres
passwd postgres
```

Please note the second step will require creating a new user password. Unless it is a personal test it's better to avoid obvious passwords like *postgres*.

In order to build binaries we must download and extract PostgreSQL's source tarball.

COMMAND

```
mkdir ~/download
cd ~/download
wget https://ftp.postgresql.org/pub/source/v11.1/postgresql-11.1.
    tar.bz2
tar xfj postgresql-11.1.tar.bz2
cd postgresql-11.1.tar.bz2
```

Using configure script's –prefix option we'll point install directory to a writable location. We can also use a directory named after the major version number. This will allow us to have different PostgreSQL versions installed without problems.

COMMAND

```
mkdir -p /home/postgres/bin/11
./configure --prefix=/home/postgres/bin/11
```

Configuration script will check all the dependencies and, if there's no error, will generate makefiles. Then we can start the build by simply running command *make*. The time required for compiling is variable and depends on the system's power. If you have a multi core processor make -j option can significantly improve build time. When the build is complete it's a good idea to run regression tests. Those tests are designed to find any regression or malfunction before the binaries are installed.

COMMAND

```
make && make check
```

The test's results are written in the source's subdirectory src/test/regress/results. If there's no error we can finalize installation with command make install.

COMMAND

```
make install
```

2.2 Packaged install

2.2.1 Debian install

The PostgreSQL Global Development Group manages a repository in order to facilitate installations on Debian based Linux distributions using Debian's packaging system.
The packages are available for both amd64 and i386 architectures.
The list of supported distributions is available on the wiki page
http://wiki.postgresql.org/wiki/Apt.

All the installation steps require root privileges, via sudo or acquiring the root login via su. Before starting to configure the repository it is necessary to import the GPG key for the package signature verification.
In a root shell simply run

COMMAND

```
wget --quiet -O - https://www.postgresql.org/media/keys/ACCC4CF8.
```

COMMAND (Cont.)

```
asc | sudo apt-key add -
```

When the key is imported create a file named pgdg.list into the directory /etc/apt/sources.d/ and add the following row.

COMMAND

```
deb http://apt.postgresql.org/pub/repos/apt/ {codename}-pgdg main
```

The distribution's codename can be found using the command lsb_release -c. e.g.

COMMAND

```
thedoctor@tardis:~$ lsb_release -c
Codename:      ascii
```

ATTENTION

Devuan releases are named after the minor planets. Devuan 2.0's code-name is ASCII and is not included in the pgdg repository. However, this release is compatible with the Debian stretch releases and therefore the codename 'stretch' can be used for retrieving the PostgreSQL packages. If you are using old, stable Jessie there's no need to change the codename as Devuan 1.0's codename is jessie.

After the repository is configured the installation is done with just:

COMMAND

```
apt-get update
apt-get install postgreql-11 postgreql-contrib-11 postgreql-client
    -11
```

The automated installation task, on first install, creates a new database cluster in the default directory /var/lib/postgresql.

2.2.2 CentOS install

Similarly to the debian repository, on the RPM based distributions is available a PostgreSQL Yum Repository which integrates with the automatic systems and patch management providing updates for all supported versions of PostgreSQL.

The supported distributions are.

- Red Hat Enterprise Linux

- CentOS

- Scientific Linux

- Oracle Linux

- Fedora

We'll now see how to install PostgreSQL on CentOS 7.

The first thing to do is to open the web page
https://www.postgresql.org/download/linux/redhat/ and using the automatic configurator grab the command for installing the RPM package with the repository setup.

In our example we are installing PostgreSQL 11 on CentOS 7 on x86_64.

COMMAND

```
yum install https://download.postgresql.org/pub/repos/yum/11/
    redhat/rhel-7-x86_64/pgdg-centos11-11-2.noarch.rpm
Loaded plugins: fastestmirror
pgdg-centos11-11-2.noarch.rpm


    | 4.8 kB 00:00:00
Examining /var/tmp/yum-root-6VOAfm/pgdg-centos11-11-2.noarch.rpm:
    pgdg-centos11-11-2.noarch
Marking /var/tmp/yum-root-6VOAfm/pgdg-centos11-11-2.noarch.rpm to
    be installed
Resolving Dependencies
--> Running transaction check
---> Package pgdg-centos11.noarch 0:11-2 will be installed
--> Finished Dependency Resolution
```

COMMAND (Cont.)

```
...
...
...

Total size: 2.7 k
Installed size: 2.7 k
Is this ok [y/d/N]: y
Downloading packages:
Running transaction check
Running transaction test
Transaction test succeeded
Running transaction
  Installing : pgdg-centos11-11-2.noarch

    1/1
  Verifying : pgdg-centos11-11-2.noarch

    1/1

Installed:
  pgdg-centos11.noarch 0:11-2
```

After the repository is configured we can install client and server packages with the following command.

COMMAND

```
yum install postgresql11 postgresql11-server
Loaded plugins: fastestmirror
Loading mirror speeds from cached hostfile
 * base: mirror.init7.net
 * extras: mirror.init7.net
 * updates: mirror.init7.net
pgdg11

    | 4.1 kB 00:00:00
```

14

COMMAND (Cont.)

```
(1/2): pgdg11/7/x86_64/primary_db

    | 141 kB 00:00:00
(2/2): pgdg11/7/x86_64/group_gz

    | 245 B 00:00:00
Resolving Dependencies
--> Running transaction check
---> Package postgresql11.x86_64 0:11.1-1PGDG.rhel7 will be
     installed
--> Processing Dependency: postgresql11-libs(x86-64) = 11.1-1PGDG.
    rhel7 for package: postgresql11-11.1-1PGDG.rhel7.x86_64
--> Processing Dependency: libicu for package: postgresql11-11.1-1
    PGDG.rhel7.x86_64
--> Processing Dependency: libpq.so.5()(64bit) for package:
    postgresql11-11.1-1PGDG.rhel7.x86_64
---> Package postgresql11-server.x86_64 0:11.1-1PGDG.rhel7 will be
      installed
--> Running transaction check
---> Package libicu.x86_64 0:50.1.2-17.el7 will be installed
---> Package postgresql11-libs.x86_64 0:11.1-1PGDG.rhel7 will be
     installed
--> Finished Dependency Resolution

Dependencies Resolved

...
...
...


Total download size: 14 M
Installed size: 53 M
Is this ok [y/d/N]: y
Downloading packages:

...
...
```

COMMAND (Cont.)

...

```
Running transaction check
Running transaction test
Transaction test succeeded
Running transaction
  Installing : libicu-50.1.2-17.el7.x86_64


     1/4
  Installing : postgresql11-libs-11.1-1PGDG.rhel7.x86_64


     2/4
  Installing : postgresql11-11.1-1PGDG.rhel7.x86_64


     3/4
  Installing : postgresql11-server-11.1-1PGDG.rhel7.x86_64


     4/4
  Verifying  : postgresql11-11.1-1PGDG.rhel7.x86_64


     1/4
  Verifying  : postgresql11-libs-11.1-1PGDG.rhel7.x86_64


     2/4
  Verifying  : libicu-50.1.2-17.el7.x86_64


     3/4
  Verifying  : postgresql11-server-11.1-1PGDG.rhel7.x86_64


     4/4

Installed:
  postgresql11.x86_64 0:11.1-1PGDG.rhel7 postgresql11-server.x86_64
      0:11.1-1PGDG.rhel7

Dependency Installed:
  libicu.x86_64 0:50.1.2-17.el7 postgresql11-libs.x86_64 0:11.1-1
```

COMMAND (Cont.)

```
    PGDG.rhel7
```

```
Complete!
```

Differently from debian, the yum package doesn't setup the cluster automatically.

In order to configure cluster and enable it for automatic start it is sufficient to run following commands.

COMMAND

```
/usr/pgsql-11/bin/postgresql-11-setup initdb
Initializing database ... OK

systemctl enable postgresql-11
Created symlink from /etc/systemd/system/multi-user.target.wants/
    postgresql-11.service to
/usr/lib/systemd/system/postgresql-11.service.

systemctl start postgresql-11
```

Chapter 3

Install structure

Depending on the installation method, the install structure is set up in a single directory or in multiple directories.

The install from source creates some subdirectories into the destination directory:

- **bin** contains the PostgreSQL binaries

- **include** contains the server's header files

- **lib** contains the shared libraries

- **share** contains the example files and the extension configurations

The packaged install method spreads the files in different directories according to the file kind.

Each of directories contain several subdirectories named after the major version. This structure is necessary for having multiple major versions on the same machine.

For example the folder /usr/lib/postgresql can have two subdirectories *10* and *11* containing binaries and libraries of each major version.

Folder	Usage
/usr/lib/postgresql/[version]/bin/	Binaries
/usr/lib/postgresql/[version]/lib/	Shared libraries
/usr/share/postgresql/[version]/	Constributed modules and extensions
/usr/doc/postgresql/postgresql[-name]-[version]/	Documentation and changelog for the package

Table 3.1: Debian folders

The debian specific utilities are stored in the directory /usr/bin/. In this directory there is also a symbolic link named like psql binary which points to the perl script
/usr/lib/share/postgresql-common/pg_wrapper. The pg_wrapper is a script which executes psql which version is determined from the files
/.postgresqlrc or /etc/postgresql-common/user_clusters.

The yum repository installs binaries into directories named after major version. For example the PostgreSQL 11 installs the files in /usr/pgsql-11. Into this directory there are three subdirectories.

Folder	Usage
/usr/pgsql-[version]/bin/	Binaries
/usr/pgsql-[version]/lib/	Shared libraries
/usr/pgsql-[version][version]/share	Man pages, extension files

Table 3.2: Yum repository folders

3.1 The core binaries

The PostgreSQL binaries can be split in two groups, the core and the wrappers alongside with the contributed modules. Let's start then with the former group.

3.1.1 postgres

This is PostgreSQL's main process. Program can be started directly or by using the pg_ctl utility. The second method is to be preferred as it offers a simpler way to control postgres process. Direct execution is the unavoidable choice when the database won't start for an old XID near to the wraparound failure. In this case the cluster can only start in single user mode to perform a cluster wide vacuum. For historical reasons there's also a symbolic link named postmaster pointing to the postgres executable.

3.1.2 pg_ctl

This utility is the simplest way for managing a PostgreSQL instance. The program reads postgres pid from cluster's data area and sends OS signals to start, stop or reload the process. It's also possible to send kill signals to the running instance. pg_ctl provides the following actions:

- **init[db]** initialises a directory as PostgreSQL data area

- **start** starts a PostgreSQL instance

- **stop** shutdowns a PostgreSQL instance

- **reload** reloads configuration's files

- **status** checks PostgreSQL instance running status

- **promote** promotes a standby server

- **kill** sends a custom signal to a running instance

In 4 we'll see how to manage the cluster.

3.1.3 initdb

Is the binary which initialises the PostgreSQL data area. The directory to initialise must be empty. Various options can be specified on the command line, like the character encoding or the collation order.

3.1.4 psql

This is the PostgreSQL command line client shipped with the PostgreSQL core distribution. At first look psql may seem very essential. However it comes with great features and flexibility.

3.1.5 pg_dump

This is the binary dedicated to backup. Can produce consistent backups in various formats. The usage is described in 10.

3.1.6 pg_restore

This program is used to restore a database by reading a binary dump made with pg_dump utility in custom or directory format. It's able to run restore in multiple jobs in order to speed up the process. The usage is described in 11

3.1.7 pg_controldata

This program can query the cluster's control file where PostgreSQL stores critical information about the cluster's activity and reliability.

3.1.8 pg_resetwal

If a WAL file becomes corrupted the cluster cannot perform a crash recovery. This leads to an unstartable cluster in case of system crash. In such catastrophic scenario there's still a way to start the cluster. Using pg_resetwal the cluster is cleared of any WAL file, the control file is initialised from scratch and the transaction's count is restarted.

The *tabula rasa* allows to start a cluster. But this comes at a cost. Any reference between the transaction progression and the data files is lost and any attempt to run DML queries will result in data corruption.

The PostgreSQL's documentation is absolutely clear about this point.

3.1.9 pg_receive_wal

pg_receive_wal is a program capable to stream WAL files over a database connection. It can be used as an alternate method for archiving WAL files. Using pg_receive_wal requires attention as WAL files might be recycled or deleted before they are streamed. Using pg_receive_wal combined with a replication slot will prevent such risk. In such scenario it is important to have the stream up and running constantly or there will be risk of filling up the pg_wal directory.

3.1.10 pg_basebackup

pg_basebackup is a program capable to stream the entire contents of a data area over a database connection using streaming replication protocol.

3.2 Wrappers

The second group of binaries is composed by the command wrappers adding command line functions already present as SQL statements.

3.2.1 The create and drop utilities

The binaries with the prefix create and drop like, createdb, createlang, createuser and dropdb, droplang, dropuser, are wrappers for the corresponding SQL functions. Each program performs the creation and the drop action on the correspondingly named object. For example createdb adds a database to the cluster and dropdb will drop the specified database.

3.2.2 clusterdb

This program performs a database wide cluster on the tables with clustered indices. The binary can run on a single table specified on the command line. In 9.6 we'll take a look to CLUSTER and VACUUM FULL.

3.2.3 reindexdb

The command does a database wide re-index. It's possible to run the command just on a table or index passing the relation's name on the command line. In 9.5 we'll take a good look at the index management.

3.2.4 vacuumdb

This binary is a wrapper for the VACUUM SQL command. This is the most important maintenance task and shouldn't be ignored. The program performs a database wide VACUUM if executed without a target relation. Alongside with a common vacuum it's possible to have the usage statistics updated on the same time.

3.2.5 vacuumlo

This binary will remove the orphaned large objects from the pg_largeobject system table. The pg_largeobject is used to store the binary objects bigger than the limit of 1GB imposed by the bytea data type. The limit for a large object is 2 GB since the version 9.2. In the version 9.3 the limit was increased to 4 TB.

3.3 Debian's specific utilities

Finally let's take a look at the Debian specific utilities. They consist of a collection of perl scripts used to simplify the cluster's management. They are installed in /usr/bin and mostly consist of symbolic links to the actual executable. We already mentioned one of them in the chapter's introduction, the psql pointing to the pg_wrapper PERL script.

3.3.1 pg_createcluster

This script adds a new PostgreSQL cluster with the given major version, if installed, and the given name. The script puts all the configuration in /etc/postgresql. Each major version has a dedicated directory within which is a group of directories containing the cluster's specific configuration files. If not specified the data directory is created in the folder /var/lib/postgresql. It's possible to specify the options for initdb.

3.3.2 pg_dropcluster

The program will delete a PostgreSQL cluster created previously with pg_createcluster. The program will not drop a running cluster. If the dropped cluster has any tablespaces those must be manually removed after the drop as the program doesn't follow the symbolic links.

3.3.3 pg_lscluster

Lists the clusters created with pg_createcluster.

3.3.4 pg_ctlcluster

The program manages the cluster in a similar way pg_ctl does. Before version 9.2 this wrapper had dangerous behavior for shutdown. The script did not offered a flexible way to provide shutdown mode. More information about shutdown sequence is in 4.3. When run without any arguments pg_ctlcluster performs a smart shutdown mode. It is possible to pass the argument -m [shutdown mode]

EXAMPLE

```
pg_ctlcluster 11 main stop -m immediate
tail /var/log/postgresql/postgresql-11-main.log
2018-12-04 07:28:14.379 EST [1415] LOG: received immediate
    shutdown request
2018-12-04 07:28:14.396 EST [1444] WARNING: terminating connection
    because of crash of another server process
```

```
2018-12-04 07:28:14.396 EST [1444] DETAIL: The postmaster has
    commanded this server process to roll back the current
    transaction and exit, because another server process exited
    abnormally and possibly corrupted shared memory.
2018-12-04 07:28:14.396 EST [1444] HINT: In a moment you should be
    able to reconnect to the database and repeat your command.
2018-12-04 07:28:14.399 EST [1415] LOG: database system is shut
    down
```

Chapter 4

Managing the cluster

A PostgreSQL cluster is made of two components: a physical location initialised as data area and the postgres processes accessing the data area and attached to a shared memory segment called shared buffer. The debian's package's installation, during first install, automatically creates a new PostgreSQL cluster in /var/lib/postgresql directory.

In order to get a better understanding of what happens under the bonnet, we'll have a look on how cluster is initialised and how it works.

4.1   Initialising the data directory

The data area is a directory that needs to be initialised by the program initdb. In order to run successfully initdb requires an empty directory for initialization. The initdb binary location depends from the installation method. We already discussed that in 3 and 2.

There are many parameters for customizing cluster's data area. If executed without any parameters initdb will initialise the data area in the location set by the environment variable PGDATA. If the variable is unset the program will exit without any further action.

For example, using the initdb shipped with the debian archive requires the following commands.

```
/usr/lib/postgresql/11/bin/initdb -k --auth-local=peer --auth-host
    =md5 -D ~/pgdata/11/main
The files belonging to this database system will be owned by user
    "postgres".
This user must also own the server process.

The database cluster will be initialised with locale "en_US.UTF
    -8".
The default database encoding has accordingly been set to "UTF8".
The default text search configuration will be set to "english".

Data page checksums are enabled.

creating directory /var/lib/postgresql/pgdata/11/main ... ok
creating subdirectories ... ok
selecting default max_connections ... 100
selecting default shared_buffers ... 128MB
selecting dynamic shared memory implementation ... posix
creating configuration files ... ok
running bootstrap script ... ok
performing post-bootstrap initialization ... ok
syncing data to disk ... ok

Success. You can now start the database server using:

    /usr/lib/postgresql/11/bin/pg_ctl -D /var/lib/postgresql/pgdata
        /11/main -l logfile start
```

Since version 9.3 PostgreSQL supports data page checksums useful for detecting data page corruption. This great feature can be enabled only when initializing data area with initdb and is applied to any database in cluster. Bear in mind that there is extra overhead caused by checksums. Extension pg_checksums allows to disable checksums, but only when PostgreSQL is stopped.

The extension's github page is available here:
https://github.com/credativ/pg_checksums.

After initializing a data directory initdb emits the message with the commands to start the database cluster. The command tells pg_ctl to redirect the output to the file logfile, hence the output of the start command is very minimal.

```
/usr/lib/postgresql/11/bin/pg_ctl -D /var/lib/postgresql/pgdata
    /11/main -l logfile start
waiting for server to start.... done
server started

cat logfile
2018-12-13 14:00:34.690 EST [1645] LOG: listening on IPv6 address
    "::1", port 5432
2018-12-13 14:00:34.690 EST [1645] LOG: listening on IPv4 address
    "127.0.0.1", port 5432
2018-12-13 14:00:34.701 EST [1645] LOG: listening on Unix socket
    "/var/run/postgresql/.s.PGSQL.5432"
2018-12-13 14:00:34.753 EST [1646] LOG: database system was shut
    down at 2018-12-13 13:58:25 EST
2018-12-13 14:00:34.772 EST [1645] LOG: database system is ready
    to accept connections
```

Removing the option -l logfile cause the server's log to be sent to the standard output.

The command stop passed to pg_ctl will shutdown the cluster.

```
/usr/lib/postgresql/11/bin/pg_ctl -D /var/lib/postgresql/pgdata
    /11/main stop

cat logfile
...
2018-12-13 14:03:27.931 EST [1645] LOG: received fast shutdown
    request
2018-12-13 14:03:27.948 EST [1645] LOG: aborting any active
    transactions
2018-12-13 14:03:27.952 EST [1645] LOG: background worker "logical
    replication launcher" (PID 1652) exited with exit code 1
2018-12-13 14:03:27.955 EST [1647] LOG: shutting down
```

4.2   The startup sequence

When PostgreSQL starts the server process allocates shared memory segment necessary for the database operations. The size of segment is set in the postgresql.conf file with the parameter shared_buffers. The default value is just 128MB.
When the memory is allocated the postgres process reads the file pg_control located in the $PGDATA/global directory in order to check if the instance requires recovery.

If the instance requires recovery then the postgres process reads the last checkpoint location from the control file and replays the data page changes from the WAL file pointed by the checkpoint location. During this process if there is any corruption on the WAL files or if the pg_control is corrupted the PostgreSQL cluster cannot be started.

After eventual recovery the postgres process starts listening on the IP addresses indicated in the parameter listen_addresses and opens the cluster for the normal activity.

4.3   The shutdown sequence

The PostgreSQL process starts the shutdown when receives an OS signal. The type of the signal determines the shutdown mode. It's possible to send the signal via the kill program or, more appropriately, using the program pg_ctl.

As seen in 3.1.2 pg_ctl the stop command accepts -m switch. This option is used to specify database shutdown mode. If it's omitted it defaults to fast which corresponds to the SIGINT signal. When shutting down fast cluster does not accepts new connections and is terminating connected backends. Any open transaction is rolled back.

The smart shutdown mode corresponds to the SIGTERM signal. With the smart shutdown cluster stops accepting new connections and waits for all backends to quit before completing the shutdown.

Both smart and fast shutdown modes leave the cluster in a clean state. In both modes before exiting the postgres process performs a final checkpoint which writes all the dirty buffers on the disk. The last checkpoint's location is also saved into the pg_control file and the cluster status is set to **shut down**.

The checkpoint can slow down the entire shutdown sequence. In particular if shared_buffer is big and contains many dirty blocks, the checkpoint can run for a very long time. Also if at the shutdown time, another checkpoint is running the postgres process will wait for this checkpoint to complete before starting the final checkpoint.

Enabling log checkpoints in the configuration gives us some visibility on what cluster is actually doing. The grand unified configuration parameter (GUC parameter) governing the setting is log_checkpoints.

If cluster doesn't stop, there is a shutdown mode which leaves cluster in dirty state. The immediate shutdown. The equivalent signal is the SIGQUIT and it causes the main process alongside with the backends to quit immediately without the checkpoint.

The subsequent start will require a crash recovery. The recovery is usually harmless with one important exception. If the cluster contains unlogged tables those relations are recreated from scratch when the recovery happens and all the data in those table is lost.
A final word about the SIGKILL signal, the dreaded kill -9. It could happen that cluster will not stop even using the immediate mode. In this case, the last resort is to use SIGKILL. Because this signal cannot be trapped in any way, the resources like shared memory and internal process semaphores will stay in place after killing the server. This will very likely affect the start of a fresh instance. Please refer to your sysadmin to find out the best way to cleanup the memory after the SIGKILL.

4.4 The processes

Alongside with postgres process there are a number of accessory processes. With a running PostgreSQL 11 cluster there are several processes associated with the main postgres process.

4.4.1 postgres: checkpointer process

As the name suggests this process take care of the cluster's checkpoint activity. A checkpoint is an important event in the cluster's life. When it starts all dirty pages in memory are written to the data files. The checkpoint frequency is regulated by the time and the number of cluster's WAL switches. The GUC (Grand Unified Configuration) parameters governing these metrics are respectively checkpoint_timeout and checkpoint_segments. There is a third parameter,
the checkpoint_completion_target which sets the percentage of the checkpoint_timeout. Cluster uses this value to spread the checkpoint over time in order to avoid disk IO spikes.

4.4.2 postgres: writer process

The background writer scans shared buffer searching for dirty pages and writes them in the data files. The process is designed to have a minimal impact on the database activity. It's possible to tune the length of a run and the delay between the writer's runs using the GUC parameters bgwriter_lru_maxpages and bgwriter_delay. They are respectively the number of dirty buffers written before the writer's sleep and the time between two runs.

4.4.3 postgres: wal writer process

This background process has been introduced with version 9.3 in order to improve efficiency of WAL writes. The process works in rounds and writes down the WAL buffers to the WAL files. The GUC parameter wal_writer_delay sets the milliseconds to sleep between the rounds.

4.4.4   postgres: autovacuum launcher process

This process is present if the autovacuum is enabled. It's purpose is to launch autovacuum backends when needed.

4.4.5   postgres: stats collector process

The process gathers database's usage statistics and stores information to the location indicated by the GUC stats_temp_directory. This is by default pg_stat_temp, a relative path to the data area.

4.4.6   postgres: logical replication launcher

Since version 10 PostgreSQL implements logical replica natively. This process is dedicated launcher for logical replication workers. When a subscriber connects to the publisher the launcher starts a new logical replication worker.

4.4.7   postgres: postgres postgres [local] idle

This is a database backend. There is a one backend for each established connection. The values after the colon show useful information. In particular between the square brackets you can find a query executed by the backend.

4.5   The memory

Externally PostgreSQL's memory structure is very simple to understand. Alongside with a single shared segment there are per user memories.

4.5.1   The shared buffer

The shared buffer, as the name suggests is segment of shared memory used by PostgreSQL to manage data pages shared across the backends. The shared buffer's size is set using the GUC parameter shared_buffers. Any change requires cluster's restart.

The memory segment is formatted in pages like the data files. When a new backend is forked from the main process it is attached to the shared buffer.

Usually the shared buffer is a fraction of the cluster's size, a simple but very efficient mechanism keeps in memory the blocks using a combination of LRU and MRU. Since version 8.3 there is a protection mechanism in place to prevent page eviction from the memory in the case of IO intensive operations.

Any data operation is performed loading the data pages in the shared buffer. Alongside with the benefits of the memory cache there is enforcement of data consistency at any time.

In particular, if any backend crash happens PostgreSQL resets all the existing connections to protect the shared buffer from potential corruption.

4.5.2   The work memory

The work memory is allocated for each connected session. Its size is set using the GUC parameter work_mem. The value can be set just for the current session using the SET statement or globally in the postgresql.conf file. Change becomes effective immediately after cluster reloads the configuration file.

A correct size for work memory can improve performance of any memory intensive operation like sorts. It's very important to set this value to a reasonable size in order to avoid any risk of out of memory error or unwanted swap.

4.5.3   The maintenance work memory

The maintenance work memory is set with parameter
maintenance_work_mem and like the work_mem is allocated for each connected session. PostgreSQL uses this memory in the maintenance operations like VACUUM or REINDEX. The value can be bigger than work_mem. In 9.1 there is more information about it. The maintenance_work_mem value can be set using the SET statement or globally in the postgresql.conf file.

4.5.4   The temporary memory

The temporary memory is set using parameter temp_buffers. The main usage is for storing temporary tables. If the table doesn't fit in the allocated memory then the relation is saved on disk. It's possible to change the temp_buffers value for the current session but only before creating a temporary table.

4.6 The data area

As seen in 4.1 data area is initialised using initdb . In this section we'll take a look to some of the PGDATA's sub directories.

4.6.1 base

This directory does what name suggests. It holds database files. For each database in the cluster there is a dedicated sub directory in base named after the database's object id. A new installation shows only three sub directories in the base directory.

Two of them are template databases: template0 and template1. The third one is postgres database. In 5 there is more information about the logical structure.

Each database directory contains many files with numerical names. They are the physical database's files, tables, indices etc.

The relation's file name is set initially using the relation's object id. Because there are operations that can change the file name (e.g. VACUUM FULL, REINDEX) PostgreSQL tracks the file name in a different pg_class's field, the relfilenode. In 7 there is more information about the physical data file structure.

4.6.2 global

The global directory holds all shared relations. Alongside with the data files there is a small file, just one data page, called pg_control. This file is vital for the cluster's activity . If there is any corruption on the control file the cluster cannot start.

4.6.3 pg_wal

This is probably the most important and critical directory in the data area. The directory holds write ahead logs, also known as WAL files. Each segment is by default 16 MB and is used to store the records for the pages changed in the shared buffer. The write first on this durable storage ensures the cluster's crash recovery. In the event of a crash WAL files are replayed when the startup begins from the last checkpoint location read from control file. Depending on database activity, there might be very heavy writes in this directory, thus putting it on separate device with high write capability, will improve overall performance of database.

4.6.4 pg_xact

This directory contains status of committed transactions stored in many files, each one big as a data page. The directory does not store status of the transactions executed with the SERIALIZABLE isolation. The directory's content is managed by PostgreSQL. The number of files is controlled by the two parameters autovacuum_freeze_max_age and vacuum_freeze_table_age. They control the "event horizon" of the oldest frozen transaction id and the pg_xact must store the commit status accordingly.

4.6.5 pg_serial

This directory is similar to the pg_clog except commit statuses are only for the transactions executed with the SERIALIZABLE isolation level.

4.6.6 pg_multixact

The directory stores statuses of multi transactions. They are used in general for the row share locks.

4.6.7 pg_notify

The directory is used to store LISTEN/NOTIFY operations.

4.6.8   pg_snapshots

This directory stores exported transaction's snapshots. Since version 9.2 PostgreSQL can export a consistent snapshot to the other sessions. More details about the snapshots are in 5.11.2.

4.6.9   pg_stat_tmp

This directory contains temporary files generated by statistic subsystem. Because the directory is constantly written, changing its location to a ramdisk might improve performance. The parameter stats_temp_directory can be changed with a simple reload.

4.6.10   pg_stat

This directory contains files saved permanently by statistic subsystem to keep them persistent between the restarts.

4.6.11   pg_subtrans

Directory contains statuses of subtransactions.

4.6.12   pg_twophase

Directory where PostgreSQL saves two phase commit's data. This feature allows a transaction to become independent from the backend status. If the backend disconnects, for example in a network outage, the transaction does not rollback, but waits for another backend to pick it up and complete the commit.

4.6.13   pg_tblspc

In this directory there are symbolic links pointing to the location of tablespaces. In 5.10 and 7.5 there is more information about it.

4.6.14 pg_replslot

From PostgreSQL 9.4 streaming or logical replication processes can be assigned to a named replication slot. The directory pg_replslot stores informations about replication slots created on the PostgreSQL cluster.

The replication slots can be physical or logical. They prevent WAL files to be recycled until the slot has been consumed. Therefore, if they are not in use, they may cause the pg_wal fill up with subsequent cluster crash.

PostgreSQL starting with version 10 supports temporary replication slots which are dropped when the consumer's session ends. Temporary replication slots are not saved on disk.

4.6.15 pg_logical

This directory stores status data for logical decoding.

Part II

Data layout

Chapter 5

The logical layout

In this chapter we'll take a look at the PostgreSQL logical layout. In order to understand what happens when the client connects, we'll start with looking at the connection process. We'll then move on to the logical aspect of relations. The end of the chapter is dedicated to tablespaces and MVCC.

5.1 The connection

When a PostgreSQL client initiates a connection, server pass trough several stages in order to determine whether to accept or reject the connection request.

First, the server checks client's connection policy using host based authentication file.
Whether the client is connecting via socket or network, its host, its login user and its network address are taken into account. The host based authentication file, pg_hba.conf, is usually present in the data area alongside the configuration file postgresql.conf.
Each row of pg_hba.conf is analyzed from the top to the bottom and first match determines authentication method applied to the request. If end of the file is reached without any match then connection is rejected.
The file pg_hba.conf is a simple text file with space separated values describing rules.

```
# TYPE DATABASE    USER          ADDRESS           METHOD

# "local" is for Unix domain socket connections only
local    all              all                           trust
# IPv4 local connections:
host     all              all       127.0.0.1/32        trust
# IPv6 local connections:
host     all              all       ::1/128             trust
# Allow replication connections from localhost, by a user with the
# replication  privilege .
local    replication      all                           trust
host     replication      all       127.0.0.1/32        trust
host     replication      all       ::1/128             trust
```

The column type specifies if the connection is local or host. The former is when the connection is made using a socket. The latter when the connection uses the network. It's also possible to specify if the host connection should be secure or plain using hostssl and hostnossl.

The Database and User columns are used to match specific databases and users.

The column address have sense only if the connection is host, hostssl or hostnossl. The value can be an IP address plus the network mask. It is also possible to specify hostname. There is full support for IPv4 and IPv6.
The pg_hba.conf's method column is the authentication method for the matched row. The action to perform after the match is done. PostgreSQL supports many methods ranging from the plain password challenge to kerberos.

pg_hba.conf can have fifth column, that's where the options for authentication method are stored. For example if choosing ldap it is possible to specify in the fifth column the search and connect options for the ldap authentication method.

Let's have a look to the most common authentication methods.

- **trust**: The connection is authorized without any further action. Quite useful if password is lost. Use it with caution.

- **peer**: The connection is authorized if an OS user matches a database user. It's useful for local connections.

- **password**: The connection establishes if a connection's user and a password matches with values stored in pg_shadow system table. This method sends password in clear text. Should be used only in trusted networks.

- **md5**: This method is similar to password. It uses a better security encoding passwords using md5 algorithm. Because md5 is deterministic, there is a pseudo random subroutine which offers a minimal protection against the risk of having the same md5 hash sent over the network.

- **scram-sha-256**: This method uses the stronger scram-sha-256 algorithm to store and exchange passwords between client and server. The method relies on SASL authentication framework.

- **reject**: The connection is rejected. This method is very useful to keep sessions out of the database, e.g. maintenance requiring single user mode.

When the connection is authorized postgres main process forks into a new backend process which is attached to the shared buffer. Fork process is expensive. It makes establishing a connection a potential bottleneck when working with applications that open and close their sessions constantly. In this case there is a concrete risk of having a performance degradation on the operating system level and eventually the risk of having zombie processes. Keeping connections constantly connected might be a reasonable fix.

However, if we have always connected clients and we run out of connections slots, and we want to increase number of max_connections parameter to allow more clients, it requires a cluster restart. For this reason alone resource planning ahead is absolutely vital.

Also, for each connection slot in max_connections postgres allocates 400 bytes of shared memory whenever it is used or not. When connection is established, postgres allocates a memory area for the connection. Its size is determined by the parameter work_mem.

By default PostgreSQL listens only on the localhost address. To add more addresses to listen it is necessary to edit parameter listen_addresses. Parameter accepts multiple listening addresses as comma separated values. It's also possible to set parameter to *. In such case cluster will listen on any addresses available on the machine.

Changing parameter listen_addresses requires a cluster restart.

5.2 Databases

Differently from other DBMS establishing a PostgreSQL connection requires database name in the connection string. Sometimes this can be omitted in psql when information is supplied in different way.

However the default assumptions made by psql can be frustrating, at first. When database name is omitted, psql checks if the environment variable $PG-DATABASE is set. If $PGDATABASE is missing then psql defaults database name to connection's username. This assumption will very likely generate an error when trying to connect to PostgreSQL.

For example, if we have a username named test but not a database named test, the connection will fail even with correct credentials.

EXAMPLE

```
psql -U test -h localhost
Password for user test:
FATAL: database "test" does not exist
```

This error appears because pg_hba.conf grants connection to our client. However check for a database name happens in next stage after password is entered. Therefore the connection is terminated when authorized client tries to connect to a not existing database.

Such error is very common when starting working with PostgreSQL. If database name to connect to is unknown, it is possible to initially connect to the postgres database created by default. Then with built-in psql command ⊔l display the list of databases within our cluster.

46

```
psql −d postgres
psql (11.1)
Type "help" for help.

db_test=# \l
                          List of databases
   Name   |  Owner   | Encoding | Collate |   Ctype    | Access privileges
----------+----------+----------+---------+------------+------------------
 db_test  | postgres | UTF8     | C       | en_GB.UTF−8 |
 postgres | postgres | UTF8     | C       | en_GB.UTF−8 |
 template0| postgres | UTF8     | C       | en_GB.UTF−8 | =c/postgres
          |          |          |         |            | postgres=CTc/postgres
 template1| postgres | UTF8     | C       | en_GB.UTF−8 | =c/postgres
          |          |          |         |            | postgres=CTc/postgres
(4 rows)
```

Database administrators coming from other DBMS can be confused by database postgres. This database has nothing special in it. Its creation was added in version 8.4 because it was useful to have it. You can just ignore it or use it for testing purposes. Dropping the database postgres doesn't corrupt cluster. Due to the common use by third party tools, before dropping it check, if is indeed not used.

The databases template0 and template1 like naming suggests are template databases. A template database is used to build new database copies via the physical file copy.

When initdb initializes data area the database template1 is generated using startup data for WAL entries, with system views and procedural language PL/PgSQL. Afterwards initdb creates databases template0 and postgres using template1 database.

The database template0 normally doesn't allow connections. Its main usage is to rebuild database template1 if it gets corrupted or if we need to create a database with a character encoding different from clusterwide settings.

```
db_test=# CREATE DATABASE db_test WITH ENCODING 'UTF8'
    LC_CTYPE 'en_US.UTF-8';
```

```
ERROR:  new LC_CTYPE (en_US.UTF-8) is incompatible with
      the LC_CTYPE of the
template database (en_GB.UTF-8)
HINT:  Use the same LC_CTYPE as in the template
    database, or use template0 as
template.

db_test=# CREATE DATABASE db_test WITH ENCODING 'UTF8'
    LC_CTYPE 'en_US.UTF-8'
TEMPLATE template0;
CREATE DATABASE
db_test=#
```

If template name is omitted then CREATE DATABASE uses database template1.

A database can be renamed or dropped with ALTER DATABASE and DROP DATABASE statements. However for executing a drop or rename it is required to have an exclusive access to the affected database. Any client connected to the database to be dropped or renamed will make the operation to fail.

```
db_test=# ALTER DATABASE db_test RENAME TO db_to_drop;
ALTER DATABASE

db_test=# DROP DATABASE db_to_drop;
DROP DATABASE
```

5.3   Tables

Inside a PostgreSQL database there are relations. In the PostgreSQL jargon a relation is an object which can access data. Whether the data is stored on durable storage or is accessible using dynamic methods is determined by the relation's kind.

Tables are fundamental storage unit for data. PostgreSQL implements several types of tables with different levels of durability.

A table is created using SQL command CREATE TABLE. When data is stored into a table it is done without predetermined order. This happens because of the MVCC implementation where a row update can change row's physical position. MVCC implementation is described in 7.6.

PostgreSQL supports four table types.

5.3.1 Logged or normal tables

The data durability is implemented in PostgreSQL with writing data changes into a write ahead log (WAL) before the changes are consolidated on a disk. Tables in PostgreSQL log their changes in the WAL by default unless the UNLOGGED clause is used at creation time.

5.3.2 Unlogged tables

An unlogged table is exactly like a logged table except for the fact that unlogged tables are not crash safe. The data is still consolidated on the data file on a regular basis. However data changes are not written in the WAL, thus improving speed of the write operations. Data stored in an unlogged table should be considered expendable. In case of crash PostgreSQL removes all the data from the unlogged tables during the recovery process. As the unlogged tables don't write their changes in the WAL they are not available on the on physical standby.

A table can be converted from logged to unlogged using alter table command. The change from logged to unlogged is almost immediate. However the reverse requires all the pages into the table to be logged into the WAL and can take long time for large relations.

Changing logged status on table is a blocking operation.

> **EXAMPLE**
>
> ```
> db_test=# \timing
> Timing is on.
> ```

```
db_test=# CREATE TABLE foo (id integer);
CREATE TABLE
Time: 5.767 ms
db_test=# INSERT INTO foo SELECT * FROM generate_series
    (1,3000000);
INSERT 0 3000000
Time: 2042.466 ms (00:02.042)
db_test=# TRUNCATE TABLE foo;
TRUNCATE TABLE
Time: 47.533 ms
db_test=# ALTER TABLE foo SET UNLOGGED;
ALTER TABLE
Time: 15.483 ms
db_test=# INSERT INTO foo SELECT * FROM generate_series
    (1,3000000);
INSERT 0 3000000
Time: 880.486 ms
db_test=# ALTER TABLE foo SET LOGGED;
ALTER TABLE
Time: 1657.931 ms (00:01.658)
```

5.3.3 Temporary tables

A temporary table is a relation created inside backend's local memory. When the connection ends the table is dropped. Temporary table names do not clash across the sessions as they are private. Temporary tables fit in memory as long as their size is smaller than the temp_buffers set for the session. If the table's size is bigger than temp_buffers the table is stored on disk. The session parameter temp_buffers can be set to a different value only before first temporary table is accessed within the session.

```
db_test=# CREATE TEMPORARY TABLE foo(id integer);
CREATE TABLE
db_test=# SET temp_buffers ='300MB';
```

5.3.4 Foreign tables

Foreign tables are supported by PostgreSQL since version 9.1. A foreign table works like a local table except for a foreign data wrapper which interacts with foreign data source and handles transparently data access in PostgreSQL database.

There are many different foreign data wrappers available from conventional databases up to exotic data sources. The postgres_fdw is available as well.

5.4 Table inheritance

PostgreSQL is an Object Relational Database Management System rather than a simple DBMS. Some of the concepts present in the object oriented programming are implemented in the PostgreSQL logic. The relations are also known as classes and the table's columns as attributes.

The table inheritance is a logical relationship between a parent table and its child tables. A child table inherits parent's attributes. However the physical storage is not shared.

Creating a parent/child structure is very simple.

```
db_test=#CREATE TABLE t_parent
                      (
                              i_id_data        integer,
                              v_data           character
                                 varying(300)
                      );

CREATE TABLE

db_test=#CREATE TABLE t_child_01
                ()
             INHERITS (t_parent)
                      ;
db_test=# \d t_parent
             Table "public.t_parent"
   Column   |           Type           | Modifiers
------------+--------------------------+-----------
 i_id_data  | integer                  |
 v_data     | character varying(300)   |
Number of child tables: 1 (Use \d+ to list them.)

db_test=# \d t_child_01
            Table "public.t_child_01"
   Column   |           Type           | Modifiers
------------+--------------------------+-----------
 i_id_data  | integer                  |
 v_data     | character varying(300)   |
Inherits: t_parent
```

The inheritance is usually defined at creation time. It's possible to enforce inheritance between two existing tables with ALTER TABLE ... INHERIT command. Two table's structure must be identical.

```
db_test=# ALTER TABLE t_child_01 NO INHERIT t_parent;
```

```
ALTER TABLE
db_test=# ALTER TABLE t_child_01 INHERIT t_parent;
ALTER TABLE
```

As physical storage is not shared then unique constraints can't be globally enforced on inheritance tree. That prevents creation of any global foreign key.

5.5 TOAST tables

The Oversize Attribute Storage Tecnique is the way PostgreSQL stores rows which are larger than the block size. Unlike other DBMS PostgreSQL doesn't allow the row to be split over multiple blocks. The TOAST tables are used by the TOAST strategies to store up to 1 GB of data per row. More details about TOAST are in 7.4.

5.6 Table partitioning

Since PostgreSQL 11 there is native support for table partitioning. Version 11 adds improvements to the model making the feature production ready.
PostgreSQL supports range, list and hash partitioning.
Details of the different strategies are available in official documentation:
https://www.postgresql.org/docs/11/ddl-partitioning.html

QUOTE

- Range Partitioning: The table is partitioned into "ranges" defined by a key column or set of columns, with no overlap between the ranges of values assigned to different partitions. For example, one might partition by date ranges, or by ranges of identifiers for particular business objects.

- List Partitioning: The table is partitioned by explicitly listing which key values appear in each partition.

- Hash Partitioning: The table is partitioned by specifying a modulus and a remainder for each partition. Each partition will hold the rows for which the hash value of the partition key divided by the specified modulus will produce the specified remainder.

PostgreSQL's declarative partitioning relies on table inheritance system which rules still apply. However there are some differences.

- CHECK and NOT NULL constraints on a partitioned table are always inherited by all the partitions. CHECK constraints marked as NO IN-HERIT cannot be created on the partitioned tables.

- A partitioned table does not have any data directly therefore using TRUNCATE ONLY on a partitioned table will always generate an error.

- Differently from the table inheritance partitions cannot have columns that are not present in the parent.

- Is not possible to drop the NOT NULL constraint on a partition's column if the constraint is present in the parent table.

The configuration parameter enable_partition_pruning determines whether the query planner's can ignore a partitioned table's partitions from query plans. The parameter controls the planner's ability to generate query plans which allows the query executor to ignore partitions during the query execution. The default is on.

5.7 Indices

An index is a structured relation. Each indexed value points to the corresponding table page where the indexed tuple is stored.

Indices can sensibly improve the speed of data access but they have a cost, which can be important, when the data is changed. Therefore it is important to understand if the index is really used.

The statistic tables like the pg_stat_all_indexes, are useful for finding out which index has its usage count close to zero.

For example this query finds all the indices in the public schema with index scan counter zero.

```
┌─ EXAMPLE ──────────────────────────────────────────────────────

  SELECT
          schemaname ,
          relname ,
          indexrelname ,
          idx_scan
  FROM
          pg_stat_all_indexes
  WHERE
                  schemaname = 'public'
          AND     idx_scan =0
  ;

   schemaname | relname | indexrelname | idx_scan
  ------------+---------+--------------+----------
   public     | foo     | pk_foo       |        0
  (1 row)

└──────────────────────────────────────────────────────
```

Maintaining the indices is fundamental for having good performances. In 9 we'll see how to do it.

PostgreSQL implements many types of indices. Keyword USING specifies index type at creation time.
The index is a not TOASTable relation therefore the max length for an indexed key is 1/3 of the page size.

```
┌─ EXAMPLE ──────────────────────────────────────────────────────

  CREATE INDEX idx_test ON t_test USING hash (t_contents
      );

└──────────────────────────────────────────────────────
```

If the clause USING is omitted the index defaults to the B-tree.

5.7.1 b-tree

The general purpose B-tree index implements the Lehman and Yao's high-concurrency B-tree management algorithm. The B-tree can handle equality and range queries returning ordered data. The indexed values are stored into the index pages with the pointers to the table's pages.

5.7.2 hash

The hash indices can handle only equality. Since version 10 they are WAL logged and therefore crash safe and accessible on the standby servers.

5.7.3 GiST

The GiST indices are the Generalized Search Tree. The GiST is a collection of indexing strategies organized under a common infrastructure. They can implement arbitrary indexing schemes like B-trees, R-trees or other. The default installation comes with set of operator classes working on two elements of geometrical data and for the nearest-neighbor searches. GiST indices do not perform an exact match. The false positives are removed with second check against table's data.

5.7.4 GIN

The GIN indices are the Generalized Inverted Indices. This kind of index is optimized for indexing the composite data types, arrays and vectors like a full text search elements or the JSONB. This index can index range data types. The GIN are exact indices, when scanned the returned set doesn't require a recheck. Updating a GIN index is expensive.

5.7.5 BRIN

A Block Range INdex is an index designed to manage large tables with a very compact structure. It's useful if the indexed columns have a natural correlation with their physical location. A BRIN index is always inexact and requires a recheck for data on the table's block ranges pointed by the index entries.

5.8 Views

A view is a relation which maps a name to a stored query. A view allows to have complex SQL stored and reused with ease. When a view is created the query definition is validated against the system catalog and all the objects used by the view are translated into their binary representation. The * if used within the query is expanded into the corresponding field's list.

An example will help to understand better this concept. We create a table and we add some data to it using the function generate_series(). Then we create a view defined as the SELECT * from the original table.

┌─ EXAMPLE ───

```
CREATE TABLE t_data
        (
                i_id            serial,
                t_content       text
        );

ALTER TABLE t_data
ADD CONSTRAINT pk_t_data PRIMARY KEY (i_id);


INSERT INTO t_data
        (
                t_content
        )
SELECT
        md5(i_counter::text)
FROM
        (
```

```
            SELECT
                        i_counter
            FROM
                        generate_series(1,200) as
                            i_counter
        ) t_series;

CREATE OR REPLACE VIEW v_data
AS
    SELECT
            *
    FROM
        t_data;
```

Selecting from the view shows that all the table's fields are in the results, however the view's definition in pg_views shows that the * has been translate in the table's field list.

```
db_test=# \x
db_test=# SELECT * FROM pg_views where viewname='v_data
    ';
-[ RECORD 1 ]--------------------
schemaname | public
viewname   | v_data
viewowner  | postgres
definition |  SELECT t_data.i_id,
           |     t_data.t_content
           |  FROM t_data;
```

If we add a new field to the table t_data then the view will not show the new field unless we recreate the view.

```
db_test=# ALTER TABLE t_data ADD COLUMN d_date date NOT
    NULL default now()::date;

 db_test=# SELECT * FROM t_data LIMIT 1;
  i_id |             t_content              |   d_date
 ------+------------------------------------+------------
     1 | c4ca4238a0b923820dcc509a6f75849b | 2014-05-21
 (1 row)


db_test=# SELECT * FROM v_data LIMIT 1;
  i_id |             t_content
 ------+------------------------------------
     1 | c4ca4238a0b923820dcc509a6f75849b
 (1 row)


CREATE OR REPLACE VIEW v_data
AS
  SELECT
         *
  FROM
        t_data;

db_test=# SELECT * FROM v_data LIMIT 1;
  i_id |             t_content              |   d_date
 ------+------------------------------------+------------
     1 | c4ca4238a0b923820dcc509a6f75849b | 2014-05-21
 (1 row)
```

A view can be replaced with command CREATE OR REPLACE. However if the definition adds new fields to the view the replace is possible only if the fields are appended to the view's list of attributes. If a table is referred by a view then dropping the table is not possible unless using the clause CAS-CADE. However, using CASCADE can be dangerous. The PostgreSQL's built in dependency system can result in a dropping more relations than expected. How table pg_depend is working and how dependencies are enforced is explained in 6.6.

Storing a complex SQL inside the database avoids overhead caused by the round trip between client and server, in particular if the SQL stamenent is large. A view can be joined with other tables or other views. However joining multiple views should be done carefully as query planner might be confused by mixing different queries resulting in execution plans with poor performance.

PostgreSQL from version 9.3 supports updatable views. However this feature is limited to the views defined as simple.

A view is defined as simple when all of the following is true.

- Does have exactly one entry in its FROM list, which must be a table or another updatable view.

- Does not contain WITH, DISTINCT, GROUP BY, HAVING,LIMIT, or OFFSET clauses at the top level.

- Does not contain set operations (UNION, INTERSECT or EXCEPT) at the top level

- All columns in the view's select list must be simple references to columns of the underlying relation. They cannot be expressions, literals or functions. System columns cannot be referenced, either.

- Columns of the underlying relation do not appear more than once in the view's select list.

- Does not have the security_barrier property.

A complex view can still be transformed in an updatable view by using triggers or rules.

5.9 Materialised views

Another feature introduced in the version 9.3 is the support for the materialized views. A materialized view is a physical snapshot of a saved query.

The view's data is static until it's refreshed using the command REFRESH
MATERIALIZED VIEW.
PostgreSQL supports concurrent refresh for materialized views.

5.10   Tablespaces

A tablespace is a logical name pointing to a physical location. This feature was
introduced with release 8.0 and its implementation haven't changed much.
From version 9.2 a new function pg_tablespace_location(tablespace_oid) returns the tablespace's physical location, from its object id.

When a new physical relation is created without specifying its tablespace, the
relation's tablespace defaults to the value set in default_tablespace. If de-
fault_tablespace is not set then the relation's tablespace defaults to pg_default
Just after an initdb, a PostgreSQL cluster contains only two system tablespaces,
the pg_default, which corresponds to the directory base inside the data area,
and pg_global, which is used for the cluster's shared objects and corresponds
to the directory global within the data area.

Creating a new tablespace is simple. The physical location must be present
and owner should be OS user owning postgres process.
For example, creating a a tablespace ts_test which points to the directory
named
/var/lib/postgresql/pg_tbs/ts_test requires a single SQL command.

```
EXAMPLE

CREATE TABLESPACE ts_test
OWNER postgres
LOCATION '/var/lib/postgresql/pg_tbs/ts_test' ;
```

Only superusers can create tablespaces. The clause OWNER is optional and
if is omitted the tablespace's owner defaults to the user which is issuing the
command. Tablespaces are cluster wide and are listed in the pg_tablespace
system table.

The clause TABLESPACE followed by the tablespace name will create new relation into specified tablespace.

EXAMPLE

```
CREATE TABLE t_ts_test
        (
                i_id serial ,
                v_value text
        )
TABLESPACE ts_test ;
```

A relation can be moved from one tablespace to another using ALTER command. The following command moves the table t_ts_test from tablespace ts_test to pg_default.

EXAMPLE

```
ALTER TABLE t_ts_test SET TABLESPACE pg_default;
```

The move operation is transaction safe but requires an exclusive lock on the affected relation. The lock prevents any other sessions to access the relation during the move. If the relation has a significant size, it could result in a prolonged time when table's data is not accessible.

The exclusive lock conflicts with any running pg_dump. Therefore a running pg_dump prevents any tablespace change for the relations affected by the dump.

A tablespace can be removed with the command DROP TABLESPACE. The drop can be done only if the tablespace does not contain relations. There is no CASCADE clause for the DROP TABLESPACE command.

EXAMPLE

```
db_test=# DROP TABLESPACE ts_test;
ERROR:  tablespace "ts_test" is not empty
```

┌─ EXAMPLE (Cont.) ──┐
```
db_test=# ALTER TABLE t_ts_test SET TABLESPACE
    pg_default;
ALTER TABLE
db_test=# DROP TABLESPACE ts_test;
DROP TABLESPACE
```
└───┘

A careful design using the tablespaces, for example putting tables and indices on different physical devices, can improve overall cluster's performance.

In 7.5 we'll take a look to how PostgreSQL implements tablespaces from the physical point of view.

5.11 Transactions

PostgreSQL implements atomicity, consistency and isolation with MVCC. The Multi Version Concurrency Controloffers high efficiency in concurrent user accesss.

The MVCC logic relies on a simple concept. When a transaction begins a write operation, it gets assigned a transaction id called XID. The XID is a 32 bit integer and is used to determine what the transaction can see using its relative position into an arbitrary timeline. All the committed data with an XID smaller than the current XID are considered in the past, therefore they are visible. All the transactions with an XID bigger than the current XID are considered in the future and therefore are invisible.

The XID comparison is made at tuple level using two system fields xmin and xmax associated with each tuple. When a new tuple is created into the field xmin is stored the XID which created the tuple. This field is also known as the insert's transaction id.
When a tuple is deleted then the xmax value is updated to XID which deleted the tuple. The xmax field is also know as the delete's transaction id. With the delete the tuple is not physically removed in order to ensure that transactions with smaller XID can still see the tuple as part of their snapshot.

Tuples visible to the current XID are called live tuples. Tuples that are no longer visible to the current XID are called dead tuples. This MVCC implementation doesn't have a field dedicated for the update. In PostgreSQL updating a tuple means inserting a new row version and marking the old one deleted within the same transaction. The update's XID is set into the new tuple version's xmin and the old tuple's xmax.

Dead tuples which are no longer required by running transactions can be removed by VACUUM. We'll see the tuple structure in 7.3.

Along with xmin and xmax there is the field cid storing the transaction's command id CID. The transaction's command progression is necessary to avoid that the operation will be executed on the same tuple multiple times preventing the database's Halloween Problem.

http://en.wikipedia.org/wiki/Halloween_Problem.

5.11.1   Transaction isolation

The SQL standard defines four levels of the transaction's isolation. Each level allows or prevents the so called transaction's anomalies.

- **dirty read**, when a transaction can access the data written by a concurrent not committed transactions.

- **non repeatable read**, when a transaction repeats a previous read and finds the data changed by another transaction which has committed since the initial read.

- **phantom read**, when a transaction executes a previous query and finds a different set of rows with the same search condition because the results were changed by another committed transactions.

The table 5.1 shows the transaction's isolation levels and which anomalies are possible or not within. PostgreSQL supports the minimum isolation level to read committed. Setting the isolation level to read uncommited does not cause an error. However, the system adjusts silently the level to read committed.

64

Isolation Level	Dirty Read	Nonrepeatable Read	Phantom Read
Read uncommitted	Possible	Possible	Possible
Read committed	Not possible	Possible	Possible
Repeatable read	Not possible	Not possible	Possible
Serializable	Not possible	Not possible	Not possible

Table 5.1: SQL Transaction isolation levels

The isolation level can be set when starting a new transaction using option
SET TRANSACTION ISOLATION LEVEL.

EXAMPLE

```
BEGIN TRANSACTION ISOLATION LEVEL { SERIALIZABLE |
    REPEATABLE READ | READ
COMMITTED | READ UNCOMMITTED };
```

It's also possible to change isolation level cluster wide changing the GUC
parameter transaction_isolation.

ATTENTION

PostgreSQL supports only READ COMMITTED, REPEATABLE READ,
SERIALIZABLE. It's possible to set the isolation level to READ UN-
COMMITTED but the system will set implicitly to READ COMMIT-
TED.

5.11.2 Snapshot exports

PostgreSQL 9.2 introduced transaction's snapshot exports. A session with an
open transaction, can export its snapshot to other sessions. The snapshot can
be imported as long as the exporting transaction is in progress. This feature
allows different backends to import a previously exported consistent snapshot
and run, queries in parallel on the same data set. The pg_dump's parallel
export capability uses this feature.

An example will make the concept better understood. Using the table created in 5.8 we connect to PostgreSQL and we start a new transaction with an isolation level set at least at REPEATABLE READ. Using the function pg_export_snapshot() we export the snapshot with its identifier.

┌─ EXAMPLE ───

```
db_test=# BEGIN TRANSACTION ISOLATION LEVEL REPEATABLE
    READ;
BEGIN
db_test=# SELECT pg_export_snapshot();
 pg_export_snapshot
--------------------
 00000003-0000000B-1
(1 row)

db_test=# SELECT count(*) FROM t_data;
 count
-------
   200
(1 row)
```

With another client we connect to the same database and remove all the rows from the table t_data table.

┌─ EXAMPLE ───

```
db_test=# DELETE FROM t_data;
DELETE 200
db_test=# SELECT count(*) FROM t_data;
 count
-------
     0
(1 row)
```

However, after importing the snapshot 00000003-0000000B-1 all the table's rows are back in place.

```
db_test=# BEGIN TRANSACTION ISOLATION LEVEL REPEATABLE
    READ;
BEGIN
db_test=# SET TRANSACTION SNAPSHOT '00000003-0000000B-1
    ';
SET
db_test=# SELECT count(*) FROM t_data;
 count
-------
   200
(1 row)
```

When exporting a snapshot it is necessary to use at least REPEATABLE READ isolation level. If we use READ COMMITTED during the snapshot export this does not generate an error. However the snapshot is discarded immediately because the READ COMMITTED creates a new snapshot for each command.

Chapter 6

Data integrity

There is only one thing worse than losing the database, it's when the data becomes useless because of inconsistencies. PostgreSQL supports several types of constraints in order to help to keep the data in good shape enforcing quality of the information stored within the database.

A constraint is used to enforce rules for the data stored into a table. The constraints can be defined as table or column constraints. The table constraints are defined at table level, just after the field's list. A column constraints are defined in the field's definition inline with the data type.

When a constraint is created the rule to enforce applies immediately. At creation time the table's data is validated against the constraint and the creation fails if there is data failing the validation.

6.1 Not null

NULL is a strange thing. When a NULL value is stored the resulting field entry is an empty object which doesn't consumes physical space. By default a field is always NULLable.

When evaluating NULL it's important to remind that the NULL acts like the mathematical zero. For example an expression where an element is NULL then the entire expression becomes NULL.

A NOT NULL constraint ensures that the affected field doesn't contain any NULL value.

Adding a NOT NULL constraint can be done when creating a table, adding a new field or altering an existing field.

EXAMPLE

```
--CREATE TABLE WITH NOT NULL
CREATE TABLE t_null
   (
     i_id            serial ,
     v_data          character varying (255) NOT NULL
   )
;
CREATE TABLE

db_test=# INSERT INTO t_null (v_data) VALUES (NULL);
ERROR:   null value in column "v_data" violates not-null
     constraint
DETAIL:  Failing row contains (1, null).

--ADD NOT NULL FIELD
db_test=# ALTER TABLE t_null
   ADD v_data_2 character varying(30) NOT NULL;
ALTER TABLE

--ADD NULLABLE FIELD AND ADDING A NOT NULL CONSTRAINT
     LATER
ALTER TABLE t_null ADD v_data_3 character varying(30);
ALTER TABLE t_null ALTER COLUMN v_data_3 SET NOT NULL;
```

If NOT NULL constraint is enforced when adding a new field on an already populated table it requires DEFAULT value to be set, otherwise the operation will fail.

```
db_test=# INSERT INTO t_null (v_data,v_data_2,v_data_3)
    VALUES ('foo','bar','foobar');
INSERT 0 1

db_test=# ALTER TABLE t_null ADD v_data_4 CHARACTER
    VARYING(30) NOT NULL;
2018-12-17 13:14:17.586 CET [7867] ERROR:  column "
    v_data_4" contains null values
2018-12-17 13:14:17.586 CET [7867] STATEMENT:  ALTER
    TABLE t_null ADD v_data_4 CHARACTER VARYING(30) NOT
    NULL;
ERROR:  column "v_data_4" contains null values
```

6.2   Primary keys

A primary key enforces the uniqueness and the NOT NULL of the values stored in the key's fields. The primary key creates an implicit unique index on the key's fields. The index creation is a blocking procedure. In 9.5 is explained a method for adding a primary key which can help to minimize the disruption.

A table can have only one primary key.

At creation time a primary key can be added using the syntax for table or column constraint's.

```
--PRIMARY KEY AS COLUMN CONSTRAINT
CREATE TABLE t_column_cons
        (
                i_id            serial PRIMARY KEY,
                v_data          character varying (255)
        )
;

--PRIMARY KEY AS TABLE CONSTRAINT
CREATE TABLE t_table_cons
        (
                i_id            serial,
                v_data          character varying (255)
                        ,
                CONSTRAINT pk_t_table_cons PRIMARY KEY(
                        i_id)
        )
;
```

When defined as column constraint the primary key's name is built using the table name with the prefix _pkey.
With the table constraint syntax it's possible to specify the constraint name and multiple attributes for the key.

The primary keys can be configured as natural keys where the field's values have a real meaning. For example a table storing the cities can have the field v_city set as primary key instead of using a surrogate key i_city_id.

```
--PRIMARY NATURAL KEY
CREATE TABLE t_cities
        (
                v_city          character varying (255)
                        ,
```

```
                CONSTRAINT pk_t_cities PRIMARY KEY (
                    v_city)
        )
    ;
```

This results in a more compact table with the key values already indexed.

6.3 Unique keys

The unique keys are very similar to the primary keys. They enforce the uniqueness using an implicit index but the NULL values are allowed.
A primary key is in fact the combination of a unique key and the NOT NULL constraint.

6.4 Foreign keys

A foreign key is a constraint enforcing referential integrity of the data across different tables.
The typical usage is when we have two tables that need to enforce a relationship like addresses and cities.

```
CREATE TABLE t_addresses
        (
                i_id_address    serial,
                v_address       character varying(255),
                v_city          character varying(255),
                CONSTRAINT pk_t_addresses PRIMARY KEY (
                    i_id_address)
        )
    ;
```

The city's name is a value shared across the addresses. Using a different table in relation with the address table is more efficient than using city's name on the same table.

```
CREATE TABLE t_addresses
        (
                i_id_address     serial,
                v_address        character varying(255),
                i_id_city        integer NOT NULL,
                CONSTRAINT pk_t_addresses PRIMARY KEY (
                    i_id_address)
        )
;

CREATE TABLE t_cities
        (
                i_id_city   serial,
                v_city      character varying(255),
                CONSTRAINT pk_t_cities PRIMARY KEY (
                    i_id_city)
        )
;
```

However we need to be sure that data stored into t_addresses is consistent with t_cities otherwise we risk to have an address with a not existing city.
A foreign key will keep the data consistent across the two tables.

```
ALTER TABLE t_addresses
  ADD CONSTRAINT fk_t_addr_to_t_city
  FOREIGN KEY (i_id_city)
  REFERENCES t_cities(i_id_city)
  ;
```

The foreign key works in two ways. When a row with an invalid i_id_city hits the table t_addresses the key is violated and the insert fails. Deleting or updating a row from the table t_cities which is still referenced in the table

74

t_addresses, violates the key and the delete fails.

At logical level the foreign key uses triggers to enforce the constraint. There are some options for setting the behavior of the FOREIGN KEYS. The referenced table can trigger actions on the referencing if the foreign keys set the action for the delete or update events. This is possible using the clauses ON DELETE and ON UPDATE. If not specified the default action is NO ACTION which checks the constraint validation only at the end of the transaction and is deferrable.
The RESTRICT action is like NO ACTION but is not deferrable. The CASCADE action cascades the event to the referred rows.
The following example shows how to create a foreign key with ON DELETE RESTRICT and ON UPDATE CASCADE.

EXAMPLE

```
ALTER TABLE t_addresses
  ADD CONSTRAINT fk_t_addr_to_t_city
  FOREIGN KEY (i_id_city)
  REFERENCES t_cities(i_id_city)
  ON UPDATE CASCADE ON DELETE RESTRICT
  ;
```

Foreign keys can be defined as not valid using is the NOT VALID clause. NOT VALID tells PostgreSQL that the data is already validated and shouldn't be checked. Therefore the constraint creation is immediate. The constraint's enforcement happens to the new table's data. It's possible to validate a not valid constraint later using the command VALIDATE CONSTRAINT.

EXAMPLE

```
db_test=#ALTER TABLE t_addresses
             ADD CONSTRAINT fk_t_addr_to_t_city
             FOREIGN KEY (i_id_city)
             REFERENCES t_cities(i_id_city)
             ON UPDATE CASCADE ON DELETE RESTRICT
             NOT VALID
```

```
                    ;
ALTER TABLE
db_test=# ALTER TABLE t_addresses VALIDATE CONSTRAINT
    fk_t_addr_to_t_city ;
ALTER TABLE
```

6.5   Check constraints

A check constraint is a custom check enforcing a specific condition for the
table's data. The definition can be a boolean expression or a user defined
function returning a boolean value. Like the foreign keys, the check accepts
NOT VALID clause.

The check is satisfied if the condition returns true or NULL. This behavior
can produce unpredictable results if not fully understood.
For example if we add a CHECK constraint on the v_address table to prevent
empty addresses we discover that the insert using just the city id succeeds
without the check violation.

```
db_test=# ALTER TABLE t_addresses
                ADD CONSTRAINT chk_t_addr_city_exists
                CHECK (length(v_address)>0)
                ;
db_test=# INSERT INTO t_cities (v_city) VALUES ('
    Brighton') RETURNING i_id_city;
 i_id_city
-----------
         1
(1 row)

INSERT 0 1
```

```
db_test=# INSERT INTO t_addresses (i_id_city) VALUES
    (1);
INSERT 0 1

db_test=# SELECT
    i_id_address,
    coalesce(v_address,'NULL VALUE') as v_address,
    i_id_city
  FROM
  t_addresses;
 i_id_address | v_address  | i_id_city
--------------+------------+-----------
            3 | NULL VALUE |         1
(1 row)
```

The field v_address does not have a default value and there is no constraint to prevent NULLs. The check constraint does not throw an error when checking the NULL value for v_address.

However, if we try to update the v_address value into an empty string the check prevents the update.

EXAMPLE

```
db_test=# UPDATE t_addresses SET v_address ='' WHERE
    i_id_address=3;
ERROR:  new row for relation "t_addresses" violates
    check constraint "chk_t_addr_city_exists"
DETAIL:  Failing row contains (3, , 1).
db_test=# UPDATE t_addresses SET v_address ='foo' WHERE
    i_id_address=3;
UPDATE 1
```

In order to have the v_address field enforced to prevent empty strings we shall change either the default value or add a NOT NULL constraint.

```
db_test=# ALTER TABLE t_addresses ALTER COLUMN
    v_address SET DEFAULT '' ;
ALTER TABLE
db_test=# ALTER TABLE t_addresses ALTER COLUMN
    v_address SET NOT NULL;
ALTER TABLE
db_test=# INSERT INTO t_addresses (i_id_city) VALUES
    (1);
ERROR:  new row for relation "t_addresses" violates
    check constraint "chk_t_addr_city_exists"
DETAIL:  Failing row contains (5, , 1).
```

6.6   The dependency system

One of the things that distinguish PostgreSQL from other database systems is the way dependencies between database objects are managed.

PostgreSQL does not allow any invalid objects like views or functions. Therefore any action that can invalidate dependent objects results in an error or it's propagated to the dependent objects.

The mechanism could be confusing at first sight. However the implementation is brilliant and gives great flexibility.

For example let's create a table and a view defined as a select from one of the table's fields.

```
db_test=# CREATE TABLE foo (id serial, bar character
    varying(30) );
CREATE TABLE

db_test=# CREATE VIEW foobar AS SELECT bar FROM foo;
CREATE VIEW
```

Adding a new column to the table is possible with no problems.

```
db_test=# ALTER TABLE foo ADD COLUMN bar2 boolean;
ALTER TABLE
```

However, the moment when we try to drop the column *bar*, the dependency system prevents that.

```
db_test=# ALTER TABLE foo DROP COLUMN bar;
ERROR:  cannot drop table foo column bar because other
    objects depend on it
DETAIL:  view foobar depends on table foo column bar
HINT:  Use DROP ... CASCADE to drop the dependent
    objects too.
```

One table to rule them all

In PostgreSQL the dependencies for the database objects are tracked in the system table *pg_depend*. There is also another system table *pg_shdepend* which tracks the dependencies for objects that are shared across all the databases present in the cluster.

The table's structure is very simple and well explained in the postgresql documentation

https://www.postgresql.org/docs/11/static/catalog-pg-depend.html

Name	Type	References	Description
classid	oid	pg_class.oid	The OID of the system catalog the dependent object is in
objid	oid	any OID column	The OID of the specific dependent object

79

Name	Type	References	Description
		Table 6.1 – *Continued from previous page*	
objsubid	int4		For a table column, this is the column number (the objid and classid refer to the table itself). For all other object types, this column is zero.
refclassid	oid	pg_class.oid	The OID of the system catalog the referenced object is in
refobjid	oid	any OID column	The OID of the specific referenced object
refobjsubid	int4		For a table column, this is the column number (the refobjid and refclassid refer to the table itself). For all other object types, this column is zero.
deptype	char		A code defining the specific semantics of this dependency relationship; see text

Table 6.1: Table pg_depend

The dependent objects are tracked using fields 'classid', 'objid' and 'objsubid'. The field 'classid' is the oid of the system relation stored in 'pg_class' where the dependent object is listed.

For example a schema will have 'classid' set to 'pg_namespace'. However for a table or a view the 'classid' will be 'pg_class' which is recursively listed in 'pg_class'.

The field 'objid' is the dependent object's oid stored in the 'classid''s relation. The field 'objsubid' is used only if the dependency includes a table's column where it stores the column number. Otherwise the value is set to zero.

The referenced objects are tracked using the fields 'refclassid', 'refobjid' and 'refobjsubid'. The fields have the same roles of the dependent's counterpart. The last field 'deptype' is used to store the semantics of the dependency.

- DEPENDENCY_NORMAL (n): A normal relationship between separately-created objects. The dependent object can be dropped without affecting the referenced object. The referenced object can only be dropped by specifying CASCADE, in which case the dependent object is dropped, too. Example: a table column has a normal dependency on its data type.

- DEPENDENCY_AUTO (a): The dependent object can be dropped separately from the referenced object, and should be automatically dropped (regardless of RESTRICT or CASCADE mode) if the referenced object is dropped. Example: a named constraint on a table is made auto dependent on the table, so that it will go away if the table is dropped.

- DEPENDENCY_INTERNAL (i): The dependent object was created as part of creation of the referenced object, and is really just a part of its internal implementation. A DROP of the dependent object will be disallowed outright (we'll tell the user to issue a DROP against the referenced object, instead). A DROP of the referenced object will be propagated through to drop the dependent object whether CASCADE is specified or not. Example: a trigger that's created to enforce a foreign-key constraint is made internally dependent on the constraint's pg_constraint entry.

- DEPENDENCY_EXTENSION (e): The dependent object is a member of the extension that is the referenced object (see pg_extension). The dependent object can be dropped only via DROP EXTENSION on the referenced object. Functionally this dependency type acts the same as an internal dependency, but it's kept separate for clarity and to simplify pg_dump.

- DEPENDENCY_AUTO_EXTENSION (x): The dependent object is not a member of the extension that is the referenced object (and so should not be ignored by pg_dump), but cannot function without it and should be dropped when the extension itself is. The dependent object may be dropped on its own as well.

- DEPENDENCY_PIN (p): There is no dependent object; this type of entry is a signal that the system itself depends on the referenced object, and so that object must never be deleted. Entries of this type are created only by initdb. The columns for the dependent object contain zeroes.

Dependencies, a practical example

The table pg_depend is useful any time we need to track the dependencies.
For example, if we need to run a batch data load and we want the best performance, a good approach is to remove any indices before performing the load. However dropping a primary key which is used in a foreign key is not possible unless we use cascade. Using DROP CASCADE can have unpredictable effects as the dependent objects are dropped implicitly.
A more sensible approach can be to use a view for generating the drop and create statements before. As the create and drop order is important the view should contain the ordering criteria for both statements.
The following example, yet not exhaustive, is a good starting point for generating the drop/create statements.

EXAMPLE

```
CREATE OR REPLACE VIEW create_drop_cons
AS
        SELECT DISTINCT
                format('ALTER TABLE %I.%I ADD
                    CONSTRAINT %I %s ;',sch.nspname,tab.
                    relname ,conname ,
                    pg_get_constraintdef(con.oid)) AS
                    concreate ,
                format('ALTER TABLE %I.%I DROP
```

```
                CONSTRAINT %I ;',sch.nspname,tab.
        relname ,conname)          AS condrop,
    CASE
            WHEN contype='p'
            THEN 0
            WHEN contype='f'
            THEN 1
    END AS create_order,
    CASE
            WHEN contype='p'
            THEN 1
            WHEN contype='f'
            THEN 0
    END AS drop_order,
    tab.relname as tablename,
    sch.nspname as schemaname

FROM
    pg_class tab
    INNER JOIN pg_namespace sch
            ON sch.oid=tab.relnamespace
    INNER JOIN pg_depend dep
            ON tab.oid=dep.refobjid
    INNER JOIN pg_constraint con
            ON
                    con.oid=dep.objid
            AND     con.connamespace=tab.
               relnamespace
            AND     con.conrelid=tab.oid
WHERE

            dep.classid::regclass='
                pg_constraint'::regclass
    AND     con.contype in ('p','f')
    AND     dep.deptype IN ('n','a')
;
```

• The FROM clause joins the tables pg_class, pg_namespace, pg_depend and pg_constraint.

- The WHERE condition filters the pg_depend's records only for classes stored into pg_constraint and only for dependency type normal and automatic. Another filter on pg_constaint ensures we are searching only primary and foreign keys.

- The SELECT clause uses the format function[1] to build the constraint's drop and create statements. In the create statements the constraint definition is generated using the function pg_get_constraintdef[2].

- Two CASE constructs are used to build the order for the drop and for the create statements.

- The fields relname and nspname are exposed by the view in order to allow us to filter by table and schema.

- The 'SELECT' clause requires a DISTINCT as multi column constraints in pg_depend will generate a duplicate data.

After the view is in place we can generate the drop and create constraints with ease.

EXAMPLE

```
db_test=# SELECT
        condrop
FROM
        create_drop_cons
WHERE
                tablename IN ('t_addresses','t_cities')
        AND     schemaname='public'
ORDER BY drop_order
;
                                condrop
-------------------------------------------------------------
 ALTER TABLE public.t_addresses DROP CONSTRAINT
```

---

[1] https://www.postgresql.org/docs/11/static/functions-string.html#FUNCTIONS-STRING-FORMAT

[2] https://www.postgresql.org/docs/11/static/functions-info.html

```
    fk_t_addr_to_t_city ;
 ALTER TABLE public.t_addresses DROP CONSTRAINT
    pk_t_addresses ;
 ALTER TABLE public.t_cities DROP CONSTRAINT
    pk_t_cities ;
(3 rows)

db_test=# SELECT
       concreate
FROM
       create_drop_cons
WHERE
               tablename IN ('t_addresses','t_cities')
       AND     schemaname='public'
ORDER BY create_order
;
                                        concreate
---------------------------------------------------
 ALTER TABLE public.t_addresses ADD CONSTRAINT
    pk_t_addresses PRIMARY KEY (i_id_address) ;
 ALTER TABLE public.t_cities ADD CONSTRAINT pk_t_cities
     PRIMARY KEY (i_id_city) ;
 ALTER TABLE public.t_addresses ADD CONSTRAINT
    fk_t_addr_to_t_city FOREIGN KEY (i_id_city)
    REFERENCES t_cities(i_id_city);
(3 rows)
```

ATTENTION

This view is just an example for showing how to use dependency system. As the create statements do not show the tablespaces for the primary keys the view should only be used as a starting point.

85

Chapter 7

The physical layout

After exploration of the logical structure we'll now dig into PostgreSQL's physical structure. We'll start looking at the data files and how they are organized. Then we'll move to the data pages down to the fundamental storage unit, the tuples. A section is dedicated to the TOAST tables. The chapter will end with the physical aspect of the tablespaces and the MVCC.

7.1 Data files

As seen in 4.6 the data files are stored by default in $PGDATA/base directory, which contains a directory per each database. The directory is named after the database's object identifier.

Inside the database directories there are many files with a numerical names. When a new relation is created the name is set initially to the relation's object identifier. However if the relation requires a file rebuild then the file name will change. Operations that will change the relation's file name are, for example, REINDEX and VACUUM FULL.

A relation can have multiple segments with maximum size of 1 GB. The segments have a numerical suffix which determines their order. The first segment created doesn't have suffix. Associated with the data files there are some additional files used by PostgreSQL for tracking data visibility, free space or used to reinitialise unlogged tables.

7.1.1 Free space map

The free space map is a segment present for the index and table's data files.
It has the same relation's name with the suffix _fsm. PostgreSQL uses this file
for tracking data of free space available in relation.

7.1.2 Visibility map

The table's data file have a visibility map file which suffix is _vm. PostgreSQL
tracks the data pages with all the tuples visible to the active transactions.
This fork is also used for the index only scans.

7.1.3 Initialisation fork

The initialisation fork is an empty file used to reinitialise unlogged relations
during crash recovery.

7.2 Pages

Each datafile is an array of elements called pages. The default page size is
8 Kb. It's possible to change the page size but only by compiling from the
sources with the new size and initialising a new data area. The table's pages
are also known as heap pages. The indices have the pages with a slightly
different structure than heap pages. At the bottom the index page has a
special space used to store the relationship between the index pages. In the
special space there are pointers to other index's pages. The figure 7.1 shows
an index page structure.

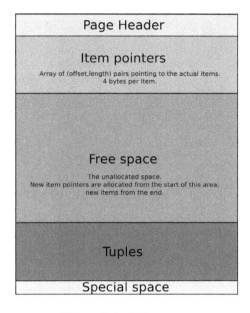

Page Header

Item pointers

Array of (offset,length) pairs pointing to the actual items.
4 bytes per item.

Free space

The unallocated space.
New item pointers are allocated from the start of this area,
new items from the end.

Tuples

Special space

Figure 7.1: Index page

A data page starts with an header long 24 bytes. After the header there are item pointers to the tuples stored in the page's bottom. The length of an item pointer is 4 bytes.

The figure 7.2 shows a page header structure.

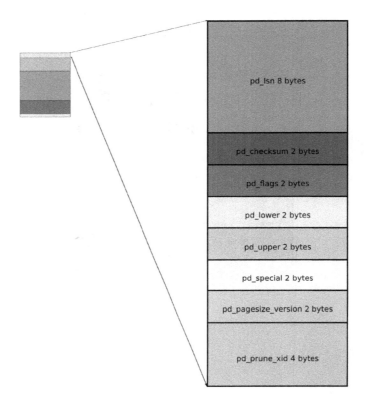

Figure 7.2: Page header

- **pd_lsn** identifies the xlog record for last page's change. This field is used by buffer manager to enforce the WAL logic. A dirty buffer is not written on disk until the WAL buffer is flushed at least as far as the buffer's LSN stored in pd_lsn.

- **pd_checksum** stores the page checksum if they are enabled

- **pd_flags** is used to store the page's various flags

90

- **pg_lower** is the offset to the start of the free space

- **pg_upper** is the offset to the end of the free space

- **pg_special** is the offset to the start of the special space if any

- **pd_pagesize_version** is the page size and the page version packed stored together in a single field.

- **pg_prune_xid** is an hint field used to determine if the tuple's pruning is useful. This field is set only on the heap pages.

The pd_checksum field replaces the pd_tli field present in the page header until PostgreSQL 9.2 which was used to track the WAL records across the timeline id.

ATTENTION

The page checksums were introduced with PostgreSQL 9.3 for detecting silent page corruption. Checksums can be enabled only when the data area is initialised with initdb.

However the third party extension pg_checksums allow to enable and disable the checksums with the cluster stopped.
https://github.com/credativ/pg_checksums

The offset fields, pg_lower, pd_upper and the optional pd_special, are 2 bytes long limiting the max page size to 32KB.

The field for the page version was introduced with PostgreSQL 7.3. Table 7.1 shows the page version number for the major versions.

7.3 Tuples

The tuples are the fundamental storage unit in PostgreSQL. They are organized as array of items which kind is initially unknown, the datum. Each tuple have a fixed header of 23 bytes as shown in the figure 7.3.

PostgreSQL version	Page version
> 8.3	4
8.1,8.2	3
8.0	2
7.4,7.3	1
< 7.3	0

Table 7.1: PostgreSQL page version

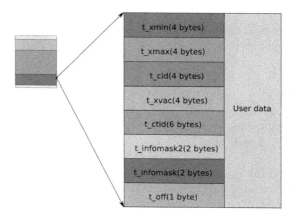

Figure 7.3: Tuple structure

The fields t_xmin and t_xmax are used to track the tuple's visibility.
The field t_cid is a "virtual" field and is used either for cmin and cmax.

The field t_xvac is used by VACUUM when moving the rows, according with the source code's comments in
src/include/access/htup_details.h this field is used only by the old style VACUUM FULL.

The field t_cid is the tuple's physical location identifier. It is composed by a couple of integers representing the page number and the tuple's index along the page. When a new tuple is created t_cid is set to the actual row's value. When the tuple is updated the value changes to the new tuple's version location. This field is used in pair with t_xmax to check if the tuple is the last version.

The two info mask fields are used to store various flags like the presence of the tuple's OID or if the tuple have NULL values.

The last field t_off is used to set the offset to the actual tuple's data. This field's value is usually zero if the table doesn't have NULLable fields and the table is created WITHOUT OIDS.

If the tuple have the OID or have NULLable fields then the object identifier and a NULL bitmap are stored immediately after the tuple's header. The bitmap if present begins just after the tuple's header and consumes enough bytes to have one bit per each data column. The OID if present is stored just after the bitmap and consumes 4 bytes.

Then there is the tuple's data, which is a datum described by the tuple's composite data type stored in the table pg_type.

7.4 TOAST

The oversize attribute storage technique is how PostgreSQL handles rows that overflow page size. PostgreSQL does not allow the tuples spanning over multiple pages. However it is possible to store large amount of data which is compressed or split in multiple rows using an external table called TOAST table. The TOAST operations are completely transparent from the user's point of view.

The storage model treats the fixed length data type and variable length data types different ways. The fixed length data types which size doesn't risk to overflow the data page are not processed through the TOAST routines. Instead data types with a variable-length (varlena) representation are TOASTable.

The TOAST strategy is stored using the first two bits[1] of the varlena length word. When both bits are zero then the attribute is an unTOASTed data type. In the remaining bits is stored the datum size in bytes including the

---

[1] On the big-endian architecture those are the high-order bits; on the little-endian those are the low-order bits

93

length word.

If the first bit is set then the value have only a single-byte header instead of the four byte header. In the remaining bits is stored the total datum size in bytes including the length byte. This scenario have a special case if the remaining bits are all zero. This means the value is a pointer to an out of line data stored in a separate TOAST table which structure is shown in figure 7.4.

Finally, whether is the first bit, if the second bit is set then the corresponding datum is compressed and must be decompressed before the use.

Because the TOAST usurps the first two bits of the varlena length word it limits the max stored size to 1 GB ($2^{30} - 1bytes$) .

First bit	Second bit	Remaining bits	Strategy
0	0	datum size in bytes including the length word	unTOASTed data type
1	0	total datum size in bytes including the length byte	toasted data type
1	0	all remaining bytes are zero	pointer to out of line in TOAST table
1	1	total datum size in bytes including the length byte	compressed toasted data type
1	1	all remaining bytes are zero	pointer to compressed out of line in TOAST table

Table 7.2: Two bits varlena length word, TOAST strategies

The toast table is composed by three fields. The chunk_id is an OID used to store the chunk identifiers. The chunk_seq is an integer which stores the chunk orders. The chunk_data is a bytea field containing the the actual data converted in a binary string.

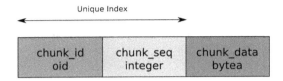

Figure 7.4: Toast table structure

The chunk size is normally 2k and is controlled at compile time by the symbol TOAST_MAX_CHUNK_SIZE. The TOAST code is triggered by the value TOAST_TUPLE_THRESHOLD, also 2k by default. When the tuple's size is bigger than
TOAST_TUPLE_THRESHOLD then the TOAST routines are triggered.

The TOAST_TUPLE_TARGET, default 2 kB, governs the compression's behavior. PostgreSQL will compress the datum to achieve a final size smaller than
TOAST_TUPLE_TARGET. Otherwise the out-of-line storage is used.
TOAST offers four different storage strategies. Each strategy can be changed per column using the ALTER TABLE SET STORAGE statement.

- PLAIN prevents either compression or out-of-line storage; It's the only storage available for fixed length data types.

- EXTENDED allows both compression and out-of-line storage. It is the default for most TOAST-able data types. Compression will be attempted first, then out-of-line storage if the row is still too big.

- EXTERNAL allows out-of-line storage but not compression.

- MAIN allows compression but not out-of-line storage. Actually the out-of-line storage is still performed as last resort.

The out of line storage has the advantage of leaving out the stored data from the row versioning; if the TOAST data is not affected by the update there will be no dead row for the TOAST data. That's possible because the varlena is a mere pointer to the chunks and a new row version will affect only the pointer leaving the TOAST data unchanged.

The TOAST table are stored like all the other relation's in the pg_class table, the associated table can be found using a self join on the field reltoastrelid.

7.5   Tablespaces

PostgreSQL implements tablespaces with help of symbolic links. Inside directory $PGDATA/pg_tblspc there are symbolic links to the physical location. Each link is named after the tablespace's OID. Therefore the tablespaces are available only on the systems with symbolic link support.

Before version 8.4 tablespace symbolic link pointed directly to the referenced directory. This was a race condition when upgrading in place because the location could clash with the upgraded cluster. Starting with version 9.0, tablespace creates a sub directory in tablespace location which is after the major version and the system catalog version number.

COMMAND

```
ls /home/postgres/data/11/tbs/ts_test/
PG_11_201809051/
```

The directory's name is a combination of the capital letters PG followed by the major version followed by the catalog version number stored in the control file.

COMMAND

```
pg_controldata
pg_control version number:        1100
Catalog version number:           201809051
Database system identifier:       6611118296419056748
```

COMMAND (Cont.)

```
Database cluster state:            in production
pg_control last modified:          Sat 22 Dec 2018 10:13:39 CET
Latest checkpoint location:        0/58184D0
Latest checkpoint's REDO location: 0/58184D0
Latest checkpoint's REDO WAL file: 000000010000000000000005
Latest checkpoint's TimeLineID:    1
Latest checkpoint's PrevTimeLineID: 1
Latest checkpoint's full_page_writes: on
Latest checkpoint's NextXID:       0:101002
Latest checkpoint's NextOID:       17093
     .
     .
     .
     .

Date/time type storage:            64-bit integers
Float4 argument passing:           by value
Float8 argument passing:           by value
Data page checksum version:        0
Mock authentication nonce:         096
     d49ce7209aa06bedfad18d53d07a87...
```

Inside the tablespace's directory the data files are organized in the same way as in the base directory.

Moving a tablespace to another physical location is possible with the cluster shut down.

After moving the tablespace to the new location is sufficient point the tablespace's symbolic link to the new physical location. After the cluster's start the new location will be used.

Until PostgreSQL 9.1 the tablespace location was stored into the field spclocation in the system table pg_tablespace.From version 9.2 the spclocation field was removed and the tablespace's location can be determined with the function
pg_tablespace_location(tablespace_oid).

This function can be used to query the system catalog about the tablespaces. In this simple example the query returns the tablespace's location resolved

97

from the OID.

```
db_test=#
                SELECT
                        pg_tablespace_location(oid),
                        spcname
                FROM
                        pg_tablespace
                ;

        pg_tablespace_location          |  spcname
-----------------------------------------+-----------
                                        |  pg_default
                                        |  pg_global
 /home/postgres/data/11/tbs/ts_test     |  ts_test
(3 rows)
```

Because the function pg_tablespace_location returns empty string for the system tablespaces, a better approach is combining the CASE construct with the function current_settings and build the absolute path for the system tablespaces.

```
db_test=# SELECT current_setting('data_directory');
        current_setting
-----------------------------------
/home/postgres/data/11/test
(1 row)

db_test=#
SELECT
  CASE
    WHEN
      pg_tablespace_location(oid)=''
      AND     spcname='pg_default'
```

```
    THEN
        current_setting('data_directory')||'/base/'
    WHEN
        pg_tablespace_location(oid)=''
        AND     spcname='pg_global'
    THEN
        current_setting('data_directory')||'/global/'
    ELSE
        pg_tablespace_location(oid)
    END
    AS      spclocation,

    spcname
FROM
    pg_tablespace;


                spclocation              |  spcname
-----------------------------------------+------------
 /home/postgres/data/11/test/base/       | pg_default
 /home/postgres/data/11/test/global/     | pg_global
 /home/postgres/data/11/tbs/ts_test      | ts_test
(3 rows)
```

7.6   MVCC

The multiversion concurrency control is the way how PostgreSQL implements the transactional model.

At logical level all seems to work by magic.

At physical level things are slightly more complicated.
When a new tuple is inserted the insert's transaction id is associated with the tuple using the tuple header's field t_xmin.
When a tuple is deleted the delete's transaction id is set into the tuple header's field t_xmax.

99

newline When a tuple is updated, the new tuple's version is inserted and the old tuple's version is deleted. The new tuple version's t_xmin is same as old version's t_xmax.

In order to determine the tuple's visibility the session's transaction id is compared with the tuple's t_xmin and t_xmax and the transaction's commit statuses.

However, because the XID is a 32 bit quantity, it can reach at most 4 billions, then it starts from 1.

When this happens theoretically all the visible tuples, with t_xmin less than the current XID, disappear because the current XID becomes less than the tuple's t_xmin.

This phenomena is called the XID wraparound failure and before PostgreSQL 7.2 was solvable with dumping the entire cluster every 4 billion transactions and reloading it into a data area created from scratch with initdb.

With PostgreSQL 7.2 new comparison method for the XID was introduced. Using the $modulo - 2^{32}$ arithmetic for each given value, there are 2 billions bigger and 2 billions smaller than the value. With this implementation the exact value of XID needs to be evaluated in terms of age.

A special XID value was also introduced, the FrozenXID[2] which is assumed always less than any other XID in the cluster and therefore always in the past.

When a tuple is created its t_xmin's age increases when new transactions are generated. When the age becomes dangerously high then VACUUM changes the ageing t_xmin with the FrozenXID, preventing the risk of having the tuple disappear.

Both pg_class and the pg_database tables have a field used to track the age of the oldest XID within themselves. However the XID value have little meaning if not analyzed with function age() which shows the number of transactions between the current XID and the value stored in the system catalog.

For example, this query returns all the databases, with their corresponding datfrozenxid and the datfrozenxid age.

---

[2]The FrozenXID's value is 2. Documentation of PostgreSQL 7.2 also mentions the BootstrapXID with value 1

When a tuple's age reaches 2 billions then the tuple simply disappears from the cluster. Before the version 8.0 there was no protection against XID wraparound failure.

Now the cluster emits warning messages if there is a database which datfrozenxid's age is less than ten million transactions from the wraparound point.

The autovacuum helps to prevent the risk of wraparound failure freezing the tables with aging tuples.

However, should the datfrozenxid reach the age of one million transactions from the wraparound point then PostgreSQL will shutdown in emergency mode refusing to accept new transactions until the risk of wraparound is removed.

Fixing the wraparound risk requires to start the postgres process in stand-alone backend and execute the VACUUM on the affected relations.

EXAMPLE

```
postgres --single -D /home/postgres/data/11/test/ postgres

PostgreSQL stand-alone backend 11.1

backend>
```

The database interface in single user mode does not have all the sophisticated features like the client psql. Anyway with a little knowledge of SQL it's possible to find the database(s) causing the shutdown and fix it.

EXAMPLE

```
backend> SELECT datname,age(datfrozenxid) FROM
    pg_database ORDER BY 2 DESC;
1: datname      (typeid = 19, len = 64, typmod = -1,
    byval = f)
2: age (typeid = 23, len = 4, typmod = -1, byval = t)
----
1: datname = "template1" (typeid = 19, len = 64, typmod
    = -1, byval = f)
2: age = "2146435072"  (typeid = 23, len = 4, typmod =
    -1, byval = t)
----
1: datname = "template0" (typeid = 19, len = 64, typmod
    = -1, byval = f)
2: age = "10"  (typeid = 23, len = 4, typmod = -1,
    byval = t)
----
1: datname = "postgres"  (typeid = 19, len = 64, typmod
    = -1, byval = f)
```

102

```
2: age = "10"  (typeid = 23, len = 4, typmod = -1,
     byval = t)
----
```

The age function shows how old is the last XID not yet frozen. In our example the database template1 has an age of 2146435072, one million transactions to the wraparound. We can then exit the backend with CTRL+D and restart it again in the single user mode specifying the database name. A VACUUM will get rid of the problematic xid.

EXAMPLE

```
postgres --single -D /home/postgres/data/11/test/ postgres

backend> SELECT current_database();
1: current_database (typeid = 19, len = 64, typmod = -1, byval = f
    )
----
1: current_database = "template1" (typeid = 19, len = 64, typmod =
     -1, byval = f)
----

backend> VACUUM FREEZE;
```

This procedure must be repeated for any database with XID near to the wraparound.

Chapter 8

Query execution

In this chapter we'll check how PostgreSQL executes a query. We'll follow the data flow from the moment where the command is sent from the backend until the results are returned to the client.

8.1 The stages of query

Any kind of query sent to the server moves across several stages before being processed. The stages have a fixed order and purpose and below we'll check them in details.

8.1.1 Syntax validation

When the client sends the query to the server it comes to the first stage, the syntax validation. This is done by the query parser. The output of the syntax validation is a "parse tree" where all the query elements are written and analysed on the syntax aspect. Any syntax error aborts the execution and the error message is returned to the client.

8.1.2 Query parsing

The parse tree is then sent to the parser, again. This time the parser transforms the parse tree into a "query tree" using the system catalogue. Each element of the parse tree is translated to the corresponding object identifier. The result is a tree where each element is uniquely associated to the to the corresponding database object.

The separation between the syntax analysis and the query to object translation is made on purpose. The reason why is that the object translation requires the parser to access the system catalogue. As the operation have a cost and requires a transaction, trapping the syntax errors before this costly operation will reduce the risk of wasting a system catalogue accesses and a transaction.

8.1.3 Query planning

The query tree is sent to the query planner which uses the internal statistics and the system catalogue to generate any possible execution plan. Each plan gets an estimated cost and the plan with the lesser cost is chosen for the execution.

The cost is an arbitrary value which value can loosely match an I/O operation. Each node plan have different costs set by estimation parameters configured in the server's configuration file.

Here a short description pulled from the PostgreSQL's pg_settings view.

- cpu_index_tuple_cost Sets the planner's estimate of the cost of processing each index entry during an index scan.

- cpu_operator_cost Sets the planner's estimate of the cost of processing each operator or function call.

- cpu_tuple_cost Sets the planner's estimate of the cost of processing each tuple (row).

- random_page_cost Sets the planner's estimate of the cost of a nonsequentially fetched disk page.

- seq_page_cost Sets the planner's estimate of the cost of a sequentially fetched disk page

- jit_above_cost Perform JIT compilation if query is more expensive.-1 disables JIT compilation.

- jit_inline_above_cost Perform JIT inlining if query is more expensive.-1 disables inlining.

106

- jit_optimize_above_cost Optimize JITed functions if query is more expensive.-1 disables optimization.

- min_parallel_index_scan_size Sets the minimum amount of index data for a parallel scan.If the planner estimates that it will read a number of index pages too small to reach this limit, a parallel scan will not be considered.

- min_parallel_table_scan_size Sets the minimum amount of table data for a parallel scan.If the planner estimates that it will read a number of table pages too small to reach this limit, a parallel scan will not be considered.

- parallel_setup_cost Sets the planner's estimate of the cost of starting up worker processes for parallel query.

- parallel_tuple_cost Sets the planner's estimate of the cost of passing each tuple (row) from worker to master backend.

- effective_cache_size Sets the planner's assumption about the total size of the data caches.That is, the total size of the caches (kernel cache and shared bu ffers) used for PostgreSQL data files. This is measured in disk pages, which are normally 8 kB each.

8.1.4   Query execution

The cheaper plan is finally sent to the executor which walks trough the plan's steps. If the query should return data then the executor sends any result to the client.
An execution plan can have different operators that are grouped two categories. The data operators and the join operators.

Figure 8.1: The query stages

8.1.5 Data operators

seq_scan

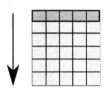

Reads sequentially the a table and discards all the rows that do not match the filter condition, if any. The operator's output is a data stream. The data is returned not ordered.

index_scan

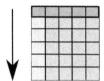

Reads an index with random disk read. For each matched tuple the corresponding table's data page is accessed and the tuple is returned. The operator returns ordered data.

index_only_scan

Reads an index with random disk read and returns the tuple without accessing the table. The operator returns ordered data.

bitmap_index/heap scan

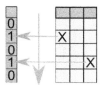

Reads the index sequentially and generates a bitmap of the occurrences. The bitmap is then used to retrieve the tuples accessing the table data pages. bitmap_index/heap scan is a good compromise between the seq_scan and a full index scan. The operator returns unsorted rows.

sort

bitmap_index/heap scan

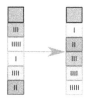

Orders the rows on a specific criteria.

8.1.6 Join operators

Nested loop

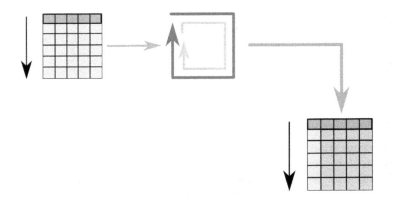

For each row returned by the operator on the left then the operator on the right is executed.

This join operator is easy to implement but can be result in slow execution on the left there is a large amount of rows and on the right an expensive operation. The best outcome is when few rows returned on the left and the operator on the right and index/index only scan.

Hash join

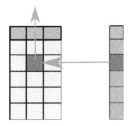

The table on the right is scanned and loaded into an hash table using its join attributes as hash keys. The operator on the left is scanned and the values of each row matching the join are used as hash keys to locate the rows within the table.

This operator doesn't require pre sorted data and can be a good choice for large joins. However the CPU can become a bottleneck if doesn't have sufficient power for the hash calculation

Merge join

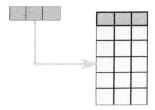

Each relation is sorted using the join attributes then the two relations are scanned in parallel. The matching rows are combined to form joined rows.

This kind of join is more attractive because each relation has to be scanned only once. However the sorts can add estra overhead which can be mitigated if the rows are sent to the operator presorted using an index on the join key.

8.2   Explain

Prepending EXPLAIN to any query will display the query's estimated execution plan . The **ANALYZE** clause executes the query, discards the results and returns the real execution plan.

```
┌─ ATTENTION ··························································
┆  Using EXPLAIN ANALYZE with the DML queries will change the data.
┆  It is safe to wrap the EXPLAIN ANALYZE between BEGIN; and ROLL-
┆  BACK;
└··········································································
```

Let consider a table containing two fields, i_id serial and v_value character varying.

```
test=# CREATE TABLE t_test
       (
               i_id    serial,
               v_value character varying(50)
       )
       ;
CREATE TABLE
```

We add add some data to the table using the function generate_series

```
test=# INSERT INTO t_test
               (v_value)
       SELECT
               v_value
       FROM
       (
               SELECT
                       generate_series(1,1000) as i_cnt,
                       md5(random()::text) as v_value
       ) t_gen
               ;
INSERT 0 1000
```

Now we can generate the estimated plan for a select return one specific row.

```
test=# EXPLAIN SELECT * FROM t_test WHERE i_id=20;
                          QUERY PLAN
------------------------------------------------
 Seq Scan on t_test  (cost=0.00..16.62 rows=3 width
    =122)
    Filter: (i_id = 20)
(2 rows)
```

112

The output of explain is simple to understand. The values within the parentheses are the estimated startup cost and the estimated total cost.
The start up cost is the cost required to deliver the first row to the next operator. The total cost is cost to deliver all the rows to the next operator. Rows and width display the expected rows to be returned by the operation and the average row width in bytes.
Using EXPLAIN ANALYZE we can generate the real execution plan.

EXAMPLE

```
test=# EXPLAIN ANALYZE SELECT * FROM t_test WHERE i_id
   =20;
                          QUERY PLAN
-----------------------------------------------
 Seq Scan on t_test  (cost=0.00..21.50 rows=1 width=37)
      (actual time=0.022..0.262 rows=1 loops=1)
   Filter: (i_id = 20)
   Rows Removed by Filter: 999
 Planning time: 0.066 ms
 Execution time: 0.286 ms
(5 rows)
```

A new set of values appear. Actual time is the startup and total time in milliseconds. Like for the costs they are respectively the time necessary to deliver one row and the time for delivering all rows to the next step. Loops specifies how many times the operator has been executed.
In our example we see that the table is scanned sequentially and 999 rows were removed by the filter.
We also get two useful information about the planning time and the execution time.
If we add an index on the field i_id the execution plan changes.

113

```
test=# CREATE INDEX idx_i_id ON t_test (i_id);
CREATE INDEX

test=# EXPLAIN ANALYZE SELECT * FROM t_test WHERE i_id
   =20;
                        QUERY PLAN
------------------------------------------------------
 Index Scan using idx_i_id on t_test  (cost=0.28..8.29
    rows=1 width=37) (actual time=0.035..0.036 rows=1
    loops=1)
   Index Cond: (i_id = 20)
 Planning time: 0.252 ms
 Execution time: 0.058 ms
(4 rows)
```

Now the query is several times faster. However the planning time increased because there is more than one execution plan to evaluate.

The cost based optimiser is very clever.

If for example we change the WHERE condition to select almost the entire table's contents then the sequential scan is used instead of the index scan.

```
test=# EXPLAIN ANALYZE SELECT * FROM t_test WHERE i_id
   >2;
                        QUERY PLAN
------------------------------------------------------
 Seq Scan on t_test  (cost=0.00..21.50 rows=999 width
    =37) (actual time=0.012..0.467 rows=998 loops=1)
   Filter: (i_id > 2)
   Rows Removed by Filter: 2
 Planning time: 0.142 ms
 Execution time: 0.652 ms
(5 rows)
```

EXAMPLE (Cont.)

```
test=# SET enable_seqscan='off';
SET
test=# EXPLAIN ANALYZE SELECT * FROM t_test WHERE i_id
    >2;

                        QUERY PLAN
---------------------------------------------
 Index Scan using idx_i_id on t_test  (cost=0.28..49.76
     rows=999 width=37) (actual time=0.029..0.544 rows
    =998 loops=1)
   Index Cond: (i_id > 2)
 Planning time: 0.145 ms
 Execution time: 0.741 ms
(4 rows)
```

Part III

Maintenance and backup

Chapter 9

Maintenance

The database maintenance is something crucial for keeping data access efficient. Building a proper maintenance plan is almost as important as having a good disaster recovery plan.

As seen in 7.6 when the rows are updated it generates new versions of affected tuples. The new version is stored using the available free space within the same page if possible. Should the page be full then the tuple will change page position. In this case also the indices need to be updated as they point to the pages rather the tuples. If the index page storing the tuple is full then finding free space is more complex than the table.

It's clear how frequent updates cause the tuples moving across the data file leaving a trail of dead tuples behind them. Despite the dead tuples are no longer visible to the new transactions, they consume physical space which cause the table and index bloat.

9.1 VACUUM

VACUUM is a PostgreSQL specific command which reclaims back the dead tuple's space. When executed without a target table, the command process all the tables within the database. A regular VACUUM have some beneficial effects.

- Removes the dead tuples and updates the free space map

- Updates the visibility map improving the index only scans

- It freezes the tuples with aging XID preventing the XID wraparound

The optional ANALYZE clause gathers the runtime statistics for processed table after they have been vacuumed.

However, VACUUM clears the space used by the dead rows and clean up the space inside the data files. The free space is not returned to the operating system unless there is a contiguous free space at the file's end and the relation is a table. In this case VACUUM runs a truncate scan that returns the contiguous space to the operating system.
Normally VACUUM have a minimum impact on the cluster's activity. However, because the pages are rewritten, during the VACUUM overall I/O activity increases.

The index pages are scanned as well and the dead tuples are also cleared. The VACUUM performances on the indices are influenced by the maintenance_work_mem setting. If the table does not have indices VACUUM will run the cleanup reading the pages sequentially. If there is any index VACUUM it will store in the maintenance work memory the tuple's references for the subsequent index cleanup. If there is not enough memory to fit all the tuples then VACUUM will stop the sequential read to execute the partial cleanup on the indices and free the maintenance work memory.

The maintenance_work_mem can significantly impact VACUUM's performance on large tables. For example lets build a simple table with 10 million rows.

EXAMPLE

```
db_test=# CREATE TABLE t_vacuum
          (
                  i_id serial,
```

```
                ts_value timestamp with time zone
                    DEFAULT clock_timestamp(),
                t_value text,
                CONSTRAINT pk_t_vacuum PRIMARY KEY  (
                    i_id)
        )
;



CREATE TABLE


db_test=# INSERT INTO t_vacuum
        (t_value)
SELECT
        md5(i_cnt::text)
FROM
(
        SELECT
                generate_series(1,1000000) as i_cnt
) t_cnt
;
INSERT 0 1000000

CREATE INDEX idx_ts_value
        ON t_vacuum USING btree (ts_value);

CREATE INDEX
```

In order to have a static environment we'll disable the table's autovacuum. We'll also increase the session's verbosity display in order to see what's happening during the VACUUM's run.

```
db_test=# ALTER TABLE t_vacuum
        SET
                (
                        autovacuum_enabled = false,
                        toast.autovacuum_enabled =
                                false
                )
;
ALTER TABLE
```

We are now executing a complete table rewrite running an UPDATE without the WHERE condition. This will create 10 millions of dead rows.

```
db_test=# UPDATE t_vacuum
        SET
                t_value = md5(clock_timestamp()::text)
;
UPDATE 1000000
```

Before running the VACUUM we'll change the maintenance_work_mem to a small value. We'll also enable the query timing.

```
db_test=# SET maintenance_work_mem ='2MB';
SET
SET client_min_messages='debug';
db_test=# \timing
Timing is on.
db_test=# VACUUM t_vacuum ;
DEBUG:   vacuuming "public.t_vacuum"
DEBUG:   scanned index "pk_t_vacuum" to remove 349297
```

```
   row versions
DETAIL:  CPU: user: 0.37 s, system: 0.07 s, elapsed:
   1.20 s
DEBUG:  scanned index "idx_ts_value" to remove 349297
   row versions
DETAIL:  CPU: user: 0.35 s, system: 0.06 s, elapsed:
   1.13 s
DEBUG:  "t_vacuum": removed 349297 row versions in 3601
    pages
DETAIL:  CPU: user: 0.06 s, system: 0.07 s, elapsed:
   1.32 s
DEBUG:  scanned index "pk_t_vacuum" to remove 349297
   row versions
DETAIL:  CPU: user: 0.21 s, system: 0.03 s, elapsed:
   0.58 s
DEBUG:  scanned index "idx_ts_value" to remove 349297
   row versions
DETAIL:  CPU: user: 0.24 s, system: 0.03 s, elapsed:
   0.59 s
DEBUG:  "t_vacuum": removed 349297 row versions in 3601
    pages
DETAIL:  CPU: user: 0.05 s, system: 0.08 s, elapsed:
   1.90 s
DEBUG:  scanned index "pk_t_vacuum" to remove 301406
   row versions
DETAIL:  CPU: user: 0.06 s, system: 0.00 s, elapsed:
   0.07 s
DEBUG:  scanned index "idx_ts_value" to remove 301406
   row versions
DETAIL:  CPU: user: 0.07 s, system: 0.00 s, elapsed:
   0.07 s
DEBUG:  "t_vacuum": removed 301406 row versions in 3108
    pages
DETAIL:  CPU: user: 0.02 s, system: 0.00 s, elapsed:
   0.27 s
DEBUG:  index "pk_t_vacuum" now contains 1000000 row
   versions in 8237 pages
```

```
DETAIL:  1000000 index row versions were removed.
0 index pages have been deleted, 0 are currently
    reusable.
CPU: user: 0.00 s, system: 0.00 s, elapsed: 0.00 s.
DEBUG:  index "idx_ts_value" now contains 1000000 row
    versions in 8237 pages
DETAIL:  1000000 index row versions were removed.
0 index pages have been deleted, 0 are currently
    reusable.
CPU: user: 0.00 s, system: 0.00 s, elapsed: 0.00 s.
DEBUG:  "t_vacuum": found 1000000 removable, 1000000
    nonremovable row versions in 20619 out of 20619
    pages
DETAIL:  0 dead row versions cannot be removed yet,
    oldest xmin: 101015
There were 0 unused item pointers.
Skipped 0 pages due to buffer pins, 0 frozen pages.
0 pages are entirely empty.
CPU: user: 1.97 s, system: 0.60 s, elapsed: 10.39 s.
DEBUG:  vacuuming "pg_toast.pg_toast_17106"
DEBUG:  index "pg_toast_17106_index" now contains 0 row
     versions in 1 pages
DETAIL:  0 index row versions were removed.
0 index pages have been deleted, 0 are currently
    reusable.
CPU: user: 0.00 s, system: 0.00 s, elapsed: 0.00 s.
DEBUG:  "pg_toast_17106": found 0 removable, 0
    nonremovable row versions in 0 out of 0 pages
DETAIL:  0 dead row versions cannot be removed yet,
    oldest xmin: 101015
There were 0 unused item pointers.
Skipped 0 pages due to buffer pins, 0 frozen pages.
0 pages are entirely empty.
CPU: user: 0.00 s, system: 0.00 s, elapsed: 0.00 s.
VACUUM
Time: 10410.501 ms (00:10.411)
```

VACUUM stores in the maintenance_work_mem an array of TCID pointers to the removed dead tuples. This is used for the index cleanup. With a small maintenance_work_mem the array can consume the entire memory causing VACUUM to pause the table scan for a partial index cleanup. The table scan then resumes. Increasing the maintenance_work_mem to 2 GB[1] the index scan goes on without pauses.

EXAMPLE

```
db_test=# SET maintenance_work_mem ='300MB';
SET
Time: 0.387 ms

db_test=# VACUUM t_vacuum ;
DEBUG:   vacuuming "public.t_vacuum"
DEBUG:   scanned index "pk_t_vacuum" to remove 999927
    row versions
DETAIL:  CPU: user: 0.52 s, system: 0.09 s, elapsed:
    1.77 s
DEBUG:   scanned index "idx_ts_value" to remove 999927
    row versions
DETAIL:  CPU: user: 0.52 s, system: 0.12 s, elapsed:
    1.76 s
DEBUG:   "t_vacuum": removed 999927 row versions in
    10311 pages
DETAIL:  CPU: user: 0.17 s, system: 0.19 s, elapsed:
    7.48 s
DEBUG:   index "pk_t_vacuum" now contains 1000000 row
    versions in 8237 pages
DETAIL:  999927 index row versions were removed.
0 index pages have been deleted, 0 are currently
    reusable.
CPU: user: 0.00 s, system: 0.00 s, elapsed: 0.00 s.
DEBUG:   index "idx_ts_value" now contains 1000000 row
    versions in 8237 pages
DETAIL:  999927 index row versions were removed.
```

---

[1]In order to have the table in the same conditions the table was cleared with a VACUUM FULL and bloated with a new update.

```
0 index pages have been deleted, 0 are currently
    reusable.
CPU: user: 0.00 s, system: 0.00 s, elapsed: 0.00 s.
DEBUG:  "t_vacuum": found 1000000 removable, 1000000
    nonremovable row versions in 20619 out of 20619
    pages
DETAIL:  0 dead row versions cannot be removed yet,
    oldest xmin: 101019
There were 150 unused item pointers.
Skipped 0 pages due to buffer pins, 0 frozen pages.
0 pages are entirely empty.
CPU: user: 1.68 s, system: 0.68 s, elapsed: 14.20 s.
DEBUG:  vacuuming "pg_toast.pg_toast_17106"
DEBUG:  "pg_toast_17106": found 0 removable, 0
    nonremovable row versions in 0 out of 0 pages
DETAIL:  0 dead row versions cannot be removed yet,
    oldest xmin: 101019
There were 0 unused item pointers.
Skipped 0 pages due to buffer pins, 0 frozen pages.
0 pages are entirely empty.
CPU: user: 0.00 s, system: 0.00 s, elapsed: 0.00 s.
VACUUM
Time: 14217.881 ms (00:14.218)
```

Without the indices VACUUM completes in the shortest time.

EXAMPLE

```
db_test=# DROP INDEX idx_ts_value ;
DROP INDEX
Time: 59.490 ms


db_test=# ALTER TABLE t_vacuum DROP CONSTRAINT
    pk_t_vacuum;
```

126

```
DEBUG:  drop auto-cascades to index pk_t_vacuum
ALTER TABLE
Time: 182.737 ms

db_test=# VACUUM t_vacuum;
DEBUG:  vacuuming "public.t_vacuum"
DEBUG:  "t_vacuum": removed 1000000 row versions in
   10309 pages
DEBUG:  "t_vacuum": found 1000000 removable, 1000000
   nonremovable row versions in 20619 out of 20619
   pages
DETAIL:  0 dead row versions cannot be removed yet,
   oldest xmin: 101022
There were 152 unused item pointers.
Skipped 0 pages due to buffer pins, 0 frozen pages.
0 pages are entirely empty.
CPU: user: 0.32 s, system: 0.07 s, elapsed: 1.81 s.
DEBUG:  vacuuming "pg_toast.pg_toast_17106"
DEBUG:  "pg_toast_17106": found 0 removable, 0
   nonremovable row versions in 0 out of 0 pages
DETAIL:  0 dead row versions cannot be removed yet,
   oldest xmin: 101022
There were 0 unused item pointers.
Skipped 0 pages due to buffer pins, 0 frozen pages.
0 pages are entirely empty.
CPU: user: 0.00 s, system: 0.00 s, elapsed: 0.00 s.
VACUUM
Time: 1828.797 ms (00:01.829)
```

Before proceeding lets put back the primary key and the index on the relation. We'll need it later.

```
db_test=# ALTER TABLE t_vacuum ADD CONSTRAINT
   pk_t_vacuum PRIMARY KEY (i_id);
DEBUG:  ALTER TABLE / ADD PRIMARY KEY will create
```

```
    implicit index "pk_t_vacuum" for table "t_vacuum"
DEBUG:  building index "pk_t_vacuum" on table "t_vacuum
   " with request for 2 parallel workers
ALTER TABLE
Time: 1044.928 ms (00:01.045)
db_test=# CREATE INDEX idx_ts_value
db_test-#          ON t_vacuum USING btree (ts_value);
DEBUG:  building index "idx_ts_value" on table "
   t_vacuum" with request for 2 parallel workers
CREATE INDEX
Time: 1020.994 ms (00:01.021)
```

The table seen in the example starts with the size about 800 MB. Running the update on any row doubles the table's size. The first VACUUM run does not shrink the table because there is no contiguous free space at the end of the table. If we update all rows after the VACUUM the new versions will use the free space in the top and a second VACUUM will truncate the table because of all dead rows present contiguously at the end of the table.

Anyway, when planning to use VACUUM, it is better to keep in mind that its main goal is to keep the table's size stable.

VACUUM also prevents the XID wraparound failure. When the oldest live tuple within a table has the t_xmin's older than the parameter vacuum_freeze_min_age, then VACUUM sets the frozen flag for the tuple preserving the XID stored in t_xmin and freezing the tuple safely in the past. Because VACUUM by default skips the pages without dead tuples some aging tuples could be skipped by the run. The parameter vacuum_freeze_table_age avoids this scenario forcing VACUUM to run in FREEZE mode when in the table the relfrozenxid's age exceeds the value.

⸜ ATTENTION ···

Vacuum freeze sets frozen flag regardless of the age. This generates more IO than the normal VACUUM as all of the tuples get frozen.

It's also possible to run a VACUUM FREEZE manually using the FREEZE clause. The command is equivalent of running VACUUM with vacuum_freeze_min_age set to zero.

9.2   The view pg_stat_progress_vacuum

Before PostgreSQL 9.6 it was difficult to track the vacuum activity. The view pg_stat_progress_vacuum were introduced to help the DBA to understand what VACUUM is doing.

Column	Type	Description
pid	integer	Process ID of backend.
datid	oid	OID of the database to which this backend is connected.
datname	name	Name of the database to which this backend is connected.
relid	oid	OID of the table being vacuumed.
phase	text	Current processing phase of vacuum. See Table 9.2.
heap_blks_total	bigint	Total number of heap blocks in the table. This number is reported as of the beginning of the scan; blocks added later will not be (and need not be) visited by this VACUUM.

Table 9.1 – *Continued from previous page*

Column	Type	Description
heap_blks_scanned	bigint	Number of heap blocks scanned. Because the visibility map is used to optimise scans, some blocks will be skipped without inspection; This counter only advances when the phase is scanning heap.
heap_blks_vacuumed	bigint	Number of heap blocks vacuumed. Unless the table has no indexes, this counter only advances when the phase is vacuuming heap. Blocks that contain no dead tuples are skipped.
index_vacuum_count	bigint	Number of completed index vacuum cycles.
max_dead_tuples	bigint	Number of dead tuples that we can store before needing to perform an index vacuum cycle, based on maintenance_work_mem.
num_dead_tuples	bigint	Number of dead tuples collected since the last index vacuum cycle.

Table 9.1: pg_stat_progress_vacuum fields

The vacuum phases are the following.

Phase	Description
initializing	VACUUM is preparing to begin scanning the heap. This phase is expected to be very brief.

Table 9.2 – *Continued from previous page*

Phase	Description
scanning heap	VACUUM is currently scanning the heap. It will prune and defragment each page if required, and possibly perform freezing activity. The heap_blks_scanned column can be used to monitor the progress of the scan.
vacuuming indexes	VACUUM is currently vacuuming the indexes. If a table has any indexes, this will happen at least once per vacuum, after the heap has been completely scanned. It may happen multiple times per vacuum if maintenance_work_mem is insufficient to store the number of dead tuples found.
vacuuming heap	VACUUM is currently vacuuming the heap. Vacuuming the heap is distinct from scanning the heap, and occurs after each instance of vacuuming indexes. If heap_blks_scanned is less than heap_blks_total, the system will return to scanning the heap after this phase is completed; otherwise, it will begin cleaning up indexes after this phase is completed.
cleaning up indexes	VACUUM is currently cleaning up indexes. This occurs after the heap has been completely scanned and all vacuuming of the indexes and the heap has been completed.

Table 9.2 – *Continued from previous page*	
Phase	Description
truncating heap	VACUUM is currently truncating the heap so as to return empty pages at the end of the relation to the operating system. This occurs after cleaning up indexes.
performing final cleanup	VACUUM is performing final cleanup. During this phase, VACUUM will vacuum the free space map, update statistics in pg_class, and report statistics to the statistics collector. When this phase is completed, VACUUM will end.

Table 9.2: VACUUM phases

9.3 Parameters controlling VACUUM

VACUUM is controlled by several GUC parameters.

9.3.1 vacuum_freeze_table_age

This parameter enables an implicit VACUUM FREEZE when the table's relfrozenxid exceeds the parameter's value. The default setting is 150 million transactions. Despite the possible values are between zero and one billion, VACUUM will silently set the effective value to the 95% of the autovacuum_freeze_max_age, reducing the possibility to have an anti-wraparound autovacuum.

9.3.2 vacuum_freeze_min_age

The parameter sets minimum age for the tuple's t_xmin to be frozen. The default is 50 million transactions. The values accepted are between zero to one billion. However VACUUM will change silently the effective value to one half of autovacuum_freeze_max_age in order to maximize the time between the forced autovacuum.

9.3.3 vacuum_multixact_freeze_table_age

VACUUM manages also the multixact ID. This identifier is used to store the row locks in the tuple's header. Because the multixact ID is a 32 bit quantity there is the same XID's issue with the wraparound failure. This parameter sets the value after that a table scan is performed. The setting is checked against the field relminmxid of the pg_class. The default is 150 million of multixacts. The accepted values are between zero and one billion. VACUUM limits the effective value to the 95% of autovacuum_multixact_freeze_max_age. This way the manual VACUUM has a chance to freeze the rows before an anti-wraparound autovacuum is triggered.

9.3.4 vacuum_multixact_freeze_min_age

Sets the minimum age in multixacts for VACUUM to replace the multixact IDs with a newer transaction ID or multixact ID, while scanning a table. The default is 5 million multixacts. The accepted values are between zero and one billion. VACUUM will silently limit the effective value to one half of autovacuum_multixact_freeze_max_age, in order to increase the time between the forced autovacuums.

9.3.5 vacuum_defer_cleanup_age

This parameter have effect only on the master in the hot standby configurations. When set to a positive value on the master, it can reduce the risk of query conflicts on the standby. Does not have effect on a standby server.

9.3.6 vacuum_cost_delay

This parameter, if set to a not zero value enables the cost based vacuum delay and sets the sleep time, in milliseconds, for VACUUM process when the cost limit exceeds. The default value is zero, which disables the cost-based vacuum delay feature.

9.3.7   vacuum_cost_limit

This parameter sets the arbitrary cost limit. VACUUM sleeps for the time set in vacuum_cost_delay when the value is reached. The default value is 200.

9.3.8   vacuum_cost_page_hit

The parameter sets the arbitrary cost for vacuuming one buffer found in the shared buffer cache. It represents the cost to lock the buffer, look up to the shared hash table and scan the content of the page. The default value is 1.

9.3.9   vacuum_cost_page_miss

This parameter sets the arbitrary cost for vacuuming a buffer not present in the shared buffer. This represents the effort to lock the buffer pool, lookup at the shared hash table, read the desired block from the disk and scan the buffer's contents. The default value is 10.

9.3.10   vacuum_cost_page_dirty

This parameter sets the arbitrary cost charged when vacuum scans a dirty buffer[2]. It represents the extra I/O required to flush the dirty block out to the disk. The default value is 20.

9.4   ANALYZE

The PostgreSQL's query optimizer builds the query execution plans using the cost estimates from the internal runtime statistics. Each step in the execution plan have an arbitrary cost used to compute the total cost of the plan. The execution plan with the minimum estimated cost then is used by the query executor. Therefore, keeping the runtime statistics is vital to keep the cluster's performance high.

The command ANALYZE gathers the relation's runtime statistics. When executed it reads randomly the data from the tables and builds the statistics which are then stored in pg_statistics system table.

---

[2]A buffer is dirty when the buffer is not yet written to the relation's data file

ANALYZE accepts the optional clause VERBOSE to increase the verbosity. It's also possible to specify a target table with column list to analyze. If the column list is omitted then ANALYZE will process all the table's columns. Omitting the table name will let ANALYZE to scan all tables in the database.

The GUC parameter default_statistics_target determines the amount of entries read by the sample. The default limit is 100. Increasing the value will cause the planner to get better estimates, in particular for the columns with the data distributed irregularly. However more accuracy have a cost. ANALYZE will spend a longer time on statistics gathering. Accurate statistics can also increase the planning time as more data need to be evaluated.

The following example will show how default_statistics_target can affect the estimates. We'll reuse the table created in 9.1. This is the result of ANALYZE VERBOSE with the default statistic target.

```
EXAMPLE

db_test=# SET default_statistics_target =1;
SET
db_test=# ANALYZE VERBOSE t_vacuum;
INFO:   analyzing "public.t_vacuum"
INFO:   "t_vacuum": scanned 300 of 20619 pages,
    containing 14259 live rows and 0 dead rows; 300 rows
    in sample, 980021 estimated total rows
ANALYZE
```

The table has 1 million rows but ANALYZE estimates the contents in just 980021 rows.

Now we'll run ANALYZE with default_statistics_target set to its maximum allowed value, 10000.

```
EXAMPLE

db_test=# SET default_statistics_target =10000;
SET
```

```
db_test=# ANALYZE VERBOSE t_vacuum;
INFO:   analyzing "public.t_vacuum"
INFO:   "t_vacuum": scanned 20619 of 20619 pages,
    containing 1000000 live rows and 0 dead rows;
    1000000 rows in sample, 1000000 estimated total rows
ANALYZE
```

This time the table's live tuples are estimated correctly.

The table pg_statistics is not intended for human reading. However, the statistics are translated in human readable format by the view pg_stats.

The rule of thumb when dealing with poorly performing queries, is to check are statistics up to date and accurate. The information is stored in view pg_stat_all_tables [3].

For example this query gets, for a certain table, the last execution of the manual and the auto vacuum alongside with the last analyze and auto analyze.

EXAMPLE

```
db_test=# \x
Expanded display is on.
db_test=# SELECT
        schemaname,
        relname,
        last_vacuum,
        last_autovacuum,
        last_analyze,
        last_autoanalyze
FROM
        pg_stat_all_tables
WHERE
        relname='t_vacuum'
```

---

[3] The subset views pg_stat_user_tables and pg_stat_sys_tables are useful to search respectively the current user and the system tables only.

```
;
-[ RECORD 1 ]----+-------------------------------
schemaname       | public
relname          | t_vacuum
last_vacuum      | 2019-01-18 15:46:31.233219+01
last_autovacuum  |
last_analyze     | 2019-01-18 16:26:01.683878+01
last_autoanalyze |
```

The statistics target is a per column setting allowing a fine grained tuning for the ANALYZE command.

```
--SET THE STATISTICS TO 1000 ON THE COLUMN i_id
ALTER TABLE t_vacuum
       ALTER COLUMN  i_id
                       SET STATISTICS 1000
;
```

The default statistic target can be changed for the current session only using the SET command. The cluster wide value is changed using the parameter in the postgresql.conf file.

9.5 REINDEX

When a tuple changes page because of an update, the corresponding index entries needs update as well. If the index page is full then tuple needs to be moved to a different index page. Because of the ordered structure which page should get the tuple must follow the relationship determined by the index type. Therefore the index is affected more by bloat than the tables.

To make things worse VACUUM is less effective with the indices because of their ordered structure. The empty pages can be recycled but only after at least two VACUUM runs. This is necessary because when index page is empty VACUUM mark the page as deleted using the next XID after the XID of vacuum, making the page virtually invisible. The second VACUUM clears the deleted pages returning them to the free pages available to the index. This behavior is made on purpose, because there might be running scans which still need to access the deleted page. The second VACUUM is then necessary to ensure that the page can be safely recycled.

When the bloat appears the index use more space than normally and the performance degrades. A periodical reindex is then necessary to keep the indices and the performances at their best.

Unfortunately REINDEX has a noticeable impact on the cluster's activity. To ensure the data is consistently read the REINDEX locks the table in read only mode.

When running a reindex may be useful to get an idea of what's happening under the hood. For example, when building a BTREE index PostgreSQL will sort the data. In that case it may be useful to display the sort progress using the GUC parameter trace_sort with the verbosity set to DEBUG.
The following example shows the output of trace_sort when reindexing a primary key.
If reindex requirement to sort the table's data doesn't fit in the maintenance_work_mem, PostgreSQL will use a disk sort in order to build new index. Increasing the maintenance_work_mem improves the reindex speed as sort will fit in memory.

EXAMPLE

```
db_test=# SET trace_sort =on;
db_test=# SET client_min_messages ='debug';

db_test=# REINDEX INDEX pk_t_vacuum ;
DEBUG:   building index "pk_t_vacuum" on table "t_vacuum
    " with request for 1 parallel worker
LOG:   begin index sort: unique = t, workMem = 32768,
    randomAccess = f
```

```
LOG:  begin index sort: unique = f, workMem = 4096,
    randomAccess = f
LOG:  begin index sort: unique = t, workMem = 32768,
    randomAccess = f
LOG:  begin index sort: unique = f, workMem = 4096,
    randomAccess = f
LOG:  performsort of worker 0 starting: CPU: user: 0.10
    s, system: 0.02 s, elapsed: 0.13 s
LOG:  performsort of worker 1 starting: CPU: user: 0.09
    s, system: 0.02 s, elapsed: 0.12 s
LOG:  worker 1 switching to external sort with 7 tapes:
    CPU: user: 0.09 s, system: 0.02 s, elapsed: 0.12 s
LOG:  worker 0 switching to external sort with 7 tapes:
    CPU: user: 0.10 s, system: 0.02 s, elapsed: 0.13 s
LOG:  worker 0 starting quicksort of run 1: CPU: user:
    0.10 s, system: 0.02 s, elapsed: 0.13 s
LOG:  worker 1 starting quicksort of run 1: CPU: user:
    0.09 s, system: 0.02 s, elapsed: 0.12 s
LOG:  worker 0 finished quicksort of run 1: CPU: user:
    0.19 s, system: 0.02 s, elapsed: 0.22 s
LOG:  worker 0 finished writing run 1 to tape 0: CPU:
    user: 0.20 s, system: 0.03 s, elapsed: 0.23 s
LOG:  worker 1 finished quicksort of run 1: CPU: user:
    0.18 s, system: 0.02 s, elapsed: 0.21 s
LOG:  performsort of worker 0 done: CPU: user: 0.20 s,
    system: 0.03 s, elapsed: 0.23 s
LOG:  performsort of worker 0 starting: CPU: user: 0.20
    s, system: 0.03 s, elapsed: 0.23 s
LOG:  worker 0 switching to external sort with 7 tapes:
    CPU: user: 0.20 s, system: 0.03 s, elapsed: 0.23 s
LOG:  worker 0 starting quicksort of run 1: CPU: user:
    0.20 s, system: 0.03 s, elapsed: 0.23 s
LOG:  worker 0 finished quicksort of run 1: CPU: user:
    0.20 s, system: 0.03 s, elapsed: 0.23 s
LOG:  worker 0 finished writing run 1 to tape 0: CPU:
    user: 0.20 s, system: 0.03 s, elapsed: 0.23 s
LOG:  performsort of worker 0 done: CPU: user: 0.20 s,
```

```
      system: 0.03 s, elapsed: 0.23 s
LOG:  parallel external sort of worker 0 ended, 1228
      disk blocks used: CPU: user: 0.20 s, system: 0.03 s,
      elapsed: 0.23 s
LOG:  parallel external sort of worker 0 ended, 1 disk
      blocks used: CPU: user: 0.20 s, system: 0.03 s,
      elapsed: 0.23 s
LOG:  begin index sort: unique = t, workMem = 65536,
      randomAccess = f
LOG:  begin index sort: unique = f, workMem = 4096,
      randomAccess = f
LOG:  worker 1 finished writing run 1 to tape 0: CPU:
      user: 0.20 s, system: 0.03 s, elapsed: 0.23 s
LOG:  performsort of worker 1 done: CPU: user: 0.20 s,
      system: 0.03 s, elapsed: 0.23 s
LOG:  performsort of worker 1 starting: CPU: user: 0.20
      s, system: 0.03 s, elapsed: 0.23 s
LOG:  worker 1 switching to external sort with 7 tapes:
      CPU: user: 0.20 s, system: 0.03 s, elapsed: 0.23 s
LOG:  worker 1 starting quicksort of run 1: CPU: user:
      0.20 s, system: 0.03 s, elapsed: 0.23 s
LOG:  worker 1 finished quicksort of run 1: CPU: user:
      0.20 s, system: 0.03 s, elapsed: 0.23 s
LOG:  worker 1 finished writing run 1 to tape 0: CPU:
      user: 0.20 s, system: 0.03 s, elapsed: 0.23 s
LOG:  performsort of worker 1 done: CPU: user: 0.20 s,
      system: 0.03 s, elapsed: 0.23 s
LOG:  parallel external sort of worker 1 ended, 1219
      disk blocks used: CPU: user: 0.20 s, system: 0.03 s,
      elapsed: 0.23 s
LOG:  parallel external sort of worker 1 ended, 1 disk
      blocks used: CPU: user: 0.20 s, system: 0.03 s,
      elapsed: 0.23 s
LOG:  unperformed parallel sort of worker -1 ended, 25
      KB used: CPU: user: 0.00 s, system: 0.00 s, elapsed:
      0.00 s
LOG:  performsort of worker -1 starting: CPU: user:
```

```
     0.00 s, system: 0.00 s, elapsed: 0.00 s
LOG:  worker -1 using 65508 KB of memory for read
     buffers among 2 input tapes
LOG:  performsort of worker -1 done (except 2-way final
     merge): CPU: user: 0.00 s, system: 0.00 s, elapsed:
     0.01 s
LOG:  parallel external sort of worker -1 ended, 2447
     disk blocks used: CPU: user: 0.09 s, system: 0.04 s,
     elapsed: 0.69 s
REINDEX
```

The reindex creates a new index file from the sorted data which is set into pg_class's.relfilenode. When the reindex's transaction commits the old file node is deleted.

From PostgreSQL 8.2 CREATE INDEX has CONCURRENTLY clause which allows to build the indices in a not blocking mode. With this method the index creation adds a new invalid index in the system catalog and then in a separate transaction starts a table scan to build the invalid index. A second table scan is executed to fix the invalid index entries and validate the index.

The concurrent index build has indeed some caveats and limitations though.

- Any problem with the table scan will make the command fail, leaving an invalid index in place. An invalid index is not usable but it still adds overhead to the DML.

- When building an unique index concurrently the uniqueness is enforced only when the second table scan starts. Some transactions might start reporting the uniqueness violation before the index becomes valid. In this case the index build fails during the second table scan and the invalid index will enforce the uniqueness regardless of its status.

- CREATE INDEX CONCURRENTLY cannot run within a transaction block.

If necessary it is possible to reindex a primary keys with the clause USING INDEX for the *ALTER TABLE table_name ADD ... CONSTRAINT* statement. If executed in a transaction block with a DROP CONSTRAINT it is

141

possible to change the constraint's index without losing the uniqueness enforcement.

```
CREATE UNIQUE INDEX pk_t_vacuum_new
                ON  t_vacuum USING BTREE (i_id);
CREATE INDEX
ALTER TABLE t_vacuum
                DROP CONSTRAINT pk_t_vacuum ,
                ADD CONSTRAINT pk_t_vacuum_new PRIMARY
                  KEY
                        USING INDEX pk_t_vacuum_new
            ;
ALTER TABLE
ALTER INDEX pk_t_vacuum_new
                RENAME TO pk_t_vacuum;
ALTER INDEX
```

The example uses a regular index build and then blocks the writes. It's also possible to build the new index concurrently.

This method cannot be used though if any foreign key references the local key.

```
CREATE TABLE t_vac_foreign
        (
                i_foreign serial ,
                i_id integer NOT NULL ,
                t_value text
        )
;
CREATE TABLE
ALTER TABLE t_vac_foreign
                ADD CONSTRAINT
                    fk_t_vac_foreign_t_vacuum_i_id
                        FOREIGN KEY (i_id)
```

142

```
                         REFERENCES t_vacuum (i_id)
                         ON DELETE CASCADE
                         ON UPDATE RESTRICT;
ALTER TABLE

CREATE UNIQUE INDEX pk_t_vacuum_new ON  t_vacuum USING
    BTREE (i_id);
CREATE INDEX
db_test=# ALTER TABLE t_vacuum
    DROP CONSTRAINT pk_t_vacuum,
    ADD CONSTRAINT pk_t_vacuum_new PRIMARY KEY  USING
        INDEX pk_t_vacuum_new;
ERROR:  cannot drop constraint pk_t_vacuum on table
    t_vacuum because other objects depend on it
DETAIL:  constraint fk_t_vac_foreign_t_vacuum_i_id on
    table t_vac_foreign depends on index pk_t_vacuum
HINT:  Use DROP ... CASCADE to drop the dependent
    objects too.
```

9.6   VACUUM FULL and CLUSTER

PostgreSQL has two commands for shrinking data files: CLUSTER and VAC-UUM FULL.

Both commands share the same portion of code and their difference is just in an extra ORDER BY performed by CLUSTER, necessary to reorder the tuples on the clustered index's order.

CLUSTER's purpose is to rebuild a completely new table with ordered over a previously specified clustered index. To tell PostgreSQL which index to use there is command *ALTER TABLE table_name CLUSTER ON index_name*.

For example, this is the verbose output of the cluster command for the table created in 9.1. The table has been clustered on the timestamp field's index.

```
SET trace_sort='on';
SET
SET client_min_messages ='debug';
SET
ALTER TABLE t_vacuum CLUSTER ON idx_ts_value ;
ALTER TABLE
CLUSTER t_vacuum;
DEBUG:  building index "pg_toast_17160_index" on table
   "pg_toast_17160" serially
LOG:  begin index sort: unique = t, workMem = 65536,
   randomAccess = f
LOG:  begin index sort: unique = f, workMem = 4096,
   randomAccess = f
LOG:  internal sort of worker -1 ended, 25 KB used: CPU
   : user: 0.00 s, system: 0.00 s, elapsed: 0.00 s
LOG:  performsort of worker -1 starting: CPU: user:
   0.00 s, system: 0.00 s, elapsed: 0.00 s
LOG:  performsort of worker -1 done: CPU: user: 0.00 s,
   system: 0.00 s, elapsed: 0.00 s
LOG:  internal sort of worker -1 ended, 25 KB used: CPU
   : user: 0.00 s, system: 0.00 s, elapsed: 0.04 s
DEBUG:  clustering "public.t_vacuum" using index scan
   on "idx_ts_value"
DEBUG:  "t_vacuum": found 0 removable, 1000000
   nonremovable row versions in 10310 pages
DETAIL:  0 dead row versions cannot be removed yet.
CPU: user: 0.42 s, system: 0.13 s, elapsed: 2.87 s.
DEBUG:  building index "idx_ts_value" on table "
   t_vacuum" with request for 1 parallel worker
LOG:  begin index sort: unique = f, workMem = 32768,
   randomAccess = f
LOG:  begin index sort: unique = f, workMem = 32768,
   randomAccess = f
LOG:  performsort of worker 0 starting: CPU: user: 0.09
   s, system: 0.00 s, elapsed: 0.11 s
LOG:  worker 0 switching to external sort with 7 tapes:
   CPU: user: 0.09 s, system: 0.00 s, elapsed: 0.11 s
```

```
LOG:  performsort of worker 1 starting: CPU: user: 0.08
    s, system: 0.01 s, elapsed: 0.10 s
LOG:  worker 1 switching to external sort with 7 tapes:
    CPU: user: 0.08 s, system: 0.01 s, elapsed: 0.10 s
LOG:  worker 0 starting quicksort of run 1: CPU: user:
    0.10 s, system: 0.00 s, elapsed: 0.11 s
LOG:  worker 1 starting quicksort of run 1: CPU: user:
    0.08 s, system: 0.01 s, elapsed: 0.10 s
LOG:  worker 1 finished quicksort of run 1: CPU: user:
    0.08 s, system: 0.01 s, elapsed: 0.10 s
LOG:  worker 0 finished quicksort of run 1: CPU: user:
    0.10 s, system: 0.00 s, elapsed: 0.11 s
LOG:  worker 0 finished writing run 1 to tape 0: CPU:
    user: 0.11 s, system: 0.01 s, elapsed: 0.12 s
LOG:  performsort of worker 0 done: CPU: user: 0.11 s,
    system: 0.01 s, elapsed: 0.13 s
LOG:  worker 1 finished writing run 1 to tape 0: CPU:
    user: 0.09 s, system: 0.02 s, elapsed: 0.11 s
LOG:  performsort of worker 1 done: CPU: user: 0.09 s,
    system: 0.02 s, elapsed: 0.11 s
LOG:  parallel external sort of worker 1 ended, 1219
    disk blocks used: CPU: user: 0.09 s, system: 0.02 s,
     elapsed: 0.12 s
LOG:  parallel external sort of worker 0 ended, 1228
    disk blocks used: CPU: user: 0.11 s, system: 0.01 s,
    elapsed: 0.13 s
LOG:  begin index sort: unique = f, workMem = 65536,
    randomAccess = f
...
...
...
LOG:  performsort of worker -1 starting: CPU: user:
    0.00 s, system: 0.00 s, elapsed: 0.00 s
LOG:  worker -1 using 65508 KB of memory for read
    buffers among 2 input tapes
LOG:  performsort of worker -1 done (except 2-way final
     merge): CPU: user: 0.00 s, system: 0.00 s, elapsed:
```

CLUSTER has different strategies to order the data. In this example the chosen strategy is the sequential scan and sort strategy. The tuples are stored into a new file node which is assigned to the relation's relfilenode. Before completing the operation the table's indices are rebuilt with a REINDEX. When the CLUSTER is complete, then the old file node is removed from the disk. The process is blocking because the relation is rebuilt from scratch and the process requires an exclusive access lock on the relation.

Another point to consider when running CLUSTER is the storage. There must be enough space to store old and new relation's data files and the eventual sort on disk.

VACUUM FULL do the same CLUSTER operation without the data sort. Therefore is faster and possibility using less space than CLUSTER.

The blocking nature of those commands has an unavoidable impact on the cluster's activity. CLUSTER and VACUUM FULL are intended for extraordinary maintenance and should be executed only when the cluster is not in use or during a maintenance window. CLUSTER and VACUUM FULL do not fix the XID wraparound failure.

146

9.7 Automatic vacuuming

The autovacuum daemon was introduced with PostgreSQL 8.0 and enabled
by default from the version 8.3. With autovacuum turned on the maintenance and the statistic gathering is done automatically by the cluster when
a relation meets specific conditions. Turning off autovacuum doesn't disable
completely the daemon because the workers are started automatically to prevent the XID and multixact ID wraparound failure, regardless of the setting.
In order to have autovacuum working the statistic collector must be enabled
with track_counts= 'on'.

The following parameters control the autovacuum behavior.

9.7.1 autovacuum

This parameter is used to enable or disable the autovacuum daemon. Changing
the setting requires the cluster's restart.

9.7.2 autovacuum_max_workers

The parameter sets the maximum number of autovacuum workers. Changing
the setting requires the cluster's restart. Each worker consumes one PostgreSQL connection slot.

9.7.3 autovacuum_naptime

The parameter sets the delay between two autovacuum runs on a specified
database. The delay is expressed in seconds and the default value is set to one
minute.

9.7.4 autovacuum_vacuum_scale_factor

The parameter specifies the fraction of the total relation's tuples that need
to be dead after the relation is processed by autovacuum. However the exact
amount of dead tuples that trigger the autovacuum is the percentage determined by autovacuum_vacuum_scale_factor plus the value set in value in au-
tovacuum_vacuum_threshold. The default value is 0.2, which means that au-

tovacuum will consider the table for autovacuum when the table's 20% (plus autovacuum_vacuum_threshold) is composed by dead tuples. This setting can be overridden for individual tables by changing the storage parameters with ALTER TABLE.

9.7.5   autovacuum_vacuum_threshold

This parameter sets the extra threshold of dead tuples to add to the value determined by autovacuum_vacuum_scale_factor. The value is used to trigger an automatic VACUUM. The default is 50 tuples. This setting can be overridden for individual tables by changing the storage parameters.

For example if we have a table with 10 million rows, with autovacuum_vacuum_threshold set to 50 and autovacuum_vacuum_scale_factor set to 0.2, the autovacuum will process the table when there are at least 2,000,050 dead tuples within the relation.

9.7.6   autovacuum_analyze_scale_factor

Works exactly like autovacuum_vacuum_scale_factor. It determines when an automatic ANALYZE is necessary. The default is 0.1, corresponding to the 10% of the table. The setting can be overridden for individual tables by changing storage parameters.

9.7.7   autovacuum_analyze_threshold

The parameter works like autovacuum_vacuum_threshold and is used to add an extra threshold to the dead tuples determined by autovacuum_analyze_scale_factor before starting an automatic ANALYZE. The default is 50 tuples. This setting can be overridden for individual tables by changing the storage parameters.

For example if we have a table with 10 million rows and autovacuum_analyze_scale_factor is set to 0.1, autovacuum_analyze_threshold set to 50, there will be an automatic ANALYZE, when the table contains at least 1,000,050 dead tuples.

9.7.8 autovacuum_freeze_max_age

The parameter sets the maximum age for the pg_class's relfrozenxid before an autovacuum freeze to prevent XID wraparound, is executed on the relation.

9.7.9 autovacuum_multixact_freeze_max_age

The parameter sets the maximum age of the table's pg_class's relminmxid before an autovacuum freeze to prevent multixact ID wraparound.

9.7.10 autovacuum_vacuum_cost_delay

The parameter sets the cost delay to use in the automatic VACUUM operations. If set to -1, the regular vacuum_cost_delay value will be used. The default value is 20 milliseconds.

9.7.11 autovacuum_vacuum_cost_limit

The parameter sets cost limit value to be used in the automatic VACUUM operations. If set to -1 then the regular vacuum_cost_limit value will be used. The default value is -1. The value is split among the running autovacuum workers. The sum of the limits of each worker never exceeds this variable. More information on cost based vacuum here 9.3.6.

Chapter 10

Backup

The hardware is subject to faults. Losing the storage means that entire data infrastructure becomes inaccessible, sometimes for good. Human errors like wrong delete or table drop must be taken into account as well. Only a solid backup strategy can prevent the data loss. There are many third party tools which help the DBA to setup a physical backup giving great flexibility to the backup strategy.

However, in this book we'll cover only the backup with pg_dump.

10.1 pg_dump at glance

As seen in 3.1.5, pg_dump is the backup utility shipped with PostgreSQL's core installation. pg_dump can make consistent snapshots of databases with minimal impact on the running cluster. If pg_dump is executed without options then it tries to connect to the local cluster using the operating system user for the authentication. If the backup starts, the dump is sent to the standard output.

It's important to understand that pg_dump works at logical level and generates a snapshot of the saved data which is not usable for point in time recovery purpose.

However, because pg_dump forces the entire database contents to be read, this

151

apparently limited tool is a powerful ally for spotting silent block corruption.
A quick look to the help gives lot of useful information.

EXAMPLE

```
pg_dump --help
pg_dump dumps a database as a text file or to other formats.

Usage:
  pg_dump [OPTION]... [DBNAME]

General options:
  -f, --file=FILENAME        output file or directory name
  -F, --format=c|d|t|p       output file format (custom, directory,
      tar,
                             plain text (default))
  -j, --jobs=NUM             use this many parallel jobs to dump
  -v, --verbose              verbose mode
  -V, --version              output version information, then exit
  -Z, --compress=0-9         compression level for compressed
      formats
  --lock-wait-timeout=TIMEOUT fail after waiting TIMEOUT for a
      table lock
  --no-sync                  do not wait for changes to be written
      safely to disk
  -?, --help                 show this help, then exit

Options controlling the output content:
  -a, --data-only            dump only the data, not the schema
  -b, --blobs                include large objects in dump
  -B, --no-blobs             exclude large objects in dump
  -c, --clean                clean (drop) database objects before
      recreating
  -C, --create               include commands to create database in
      dump
  -E, --encoding=ENCODING    dump the data in encoding ENCODING
  -n, --schema=SCHEMA        dump the named schema(s) only
  -N, --exclude-schema=SCHEMA do NOT dump the named schema(s)
  -o, --oids                 include OIDs in dump
```

152

```
-O, --no-owner              skip restoration of object ownership
    in
                            plain-text format
-s, --schema-only           dump only the schema, no data
-S, --superuser=NAME        superuser user name to use in plain-
    text format
-t, --table=TABLE           dump the named table(s) only
-T, --exclude-table=TABLE do NOT dump the named table(s)
-x, --no-privileges         do not dump privileges (grant/revoke)
--binary-upgrade            for use by upgrade utilities only
--column-inserts            dump data as INSERT commands with
    column names
--disable-dollar-quoting  disable dollar quoting, use SQL
    standard quoting
--disable-triggers          disable triggers during data-only
    restore
--enable-row-security       enable row security (dump only content
     user has
                            access to)
--exclude-table-data=TABLE do NOT dump data for the named table(s
    )
--if-exists                 use IF EXISTS when dropping objects
--inserts                   dump data as INSERT commands, rather
    than COPY
--load-via-partition-root load partitions via the root table
--no-comments               do not dump comments
--no-publications           do not dump publications
--no-security-labels        do not dump security label assignments
--no-subscriptions          do not dump subscriptions
--no-synchronized-snapshots do not use synchronized snapshots in
    parallel jobs
--no-tablespaces            do not dump tablespace assignments
--no-unlogged-table-data  do not dump unlogged table data
--quote-all-identifiers     quote all identifiers, even if not key
    words
--section=SECTION           dump named section (pre-data, data, or
    post-data)
```

```
┌─ EXAMPLE (Cont.) ─────────────────────────────────────────────┐
│                                                                 │
│ --serializable-deferrable wait until the dump can run without   │
│     anomalies                                                   │
│ --snapshot=SNAPSHOT          use given snapshot for the dump     │
│ --strict-names               require table and/or schema include│
│     patterns to                                                 │
│                              match at least one entity each     │
│ --use-set-session-authorization                                 │
│                              use SET SESSION AUTHORIZATION commands│
│                                   instead of                    │
│                              ALTER OWNER commands to set ownership│
│                                                                 │
│ Connection options:                                             │
│   -d, --dbname=DBNAME      database to dump                      │
│   -h, --host=HOSTNAME      database server host or socket directory│
│   -p, --port=PORT          database server port number          │
│   -U, --username=NAME      connect as specified database user   │
│   -w, --no-password        never prompt for password            │
│   -W, --password           force password prompt (should happen │
│       automatically)                                            │
│   --role=ROLENAME          do SET ROLE before dump              │
│                                                                 │
│ If no database name is supplied, then the PGDATABASE environment│
│ variable value is used.                                         │
│                                                                 │
│ Report bugs to <pgsql-bugs@postgresql.org>.                     │
│                                                                 │
└─────────────────────────────────────────────────────────────┘
```

10.1.1 Connection options

The connection options are used to specify the way pg_dump shall connect to the cluster. All the options are straightforward except for the password.

- -d, –dbname=DBNAME specifies the database to dump

- -h, –host=HOSTNAME specifies the database server's host or the socket directory

- -p, –port=PORT set the database server port number

154

- -U, –username=NAME sets the database username to use for the connection

- -w, –no-password never prompt for password

- -W, –password force the password prompt

- –role=ROLENAME execute a SET ROLE before running the dump

Normally the PostgreSQL clients don't accept passwords as parameter. However it is still possible to automate connection without specifying password by using the password file.

The password file .pgpass is a text file saved in the user's home directory and accessible by the user. Any permissive access will prevent the PostgreSQL client to read it.
In the password file each line specifies a connection using a fixed format.

EXAMPLE

hostname : port : database : username : password

The following example specifies the password to use for the connection to the host tardis on the port 5432 to the database db_test using the login user usr_test.

EXAMPLE

tardis :5432: db_test : usr_test : testpwd

10.1.2   General options

The general options are used to control the backup's output and format.

- -f followed by the FILENAME sets the file where to save the backup.

- -F followed by the format sets the backup output format. The allowed formats are *c d t p* respectively *custom directory tar plain*. The default format is plain.

- -j option specifies the number of jobs to run in parallel when dumping the data. In order to get a consistent view for each worker pg_dump uses transaction's snapshot export seen in 5.11.2. Using multiple workers requires the backup format to be directory.

- -Z sets the compression level for the compressed formats. The default is 5 resulting in a dumped archive from 5 to 8 times smaller than the original database.

- –lock-wait-timeout sets the number of milliseconds for the table lock to be acquired. If the lock wait expires before the lock is granted then the backup fails. This option is useful for avoiding to have pg_dump waiting forever for a table lock.

10.1.3 Output options

The output options are used to control the output of the backup.

- -a enables the export for only the data without the structure

- -n dumps the named schema only. It's possible to specify multiple -n switches to select many schema or using the wildcards

- -N excludes the named schema from the dump. It's possible to specify multiple schema with multiple -N switches.

- -b enables the export of the large objects. It's enabled by default unless the option -n is used

- -c adds the drop for the database objects before recreating them. this option is useful when dumping in plain mode.

- -C adds the CREATE DATABASE in the dump. this option is useful when dumping in plain mode.

- -E specifies the character encoding for the archive. Its default is the database's character encoding.

- -o include the OIDs in the dump.

- -O do not dump the restoration of the object ownership in plain-text format

- -s dump only the schema definition

- -S superuser name to use for performing high privilege actions when the dump is in plain-text format

- -t dump the named table only. It's possible to specify multiple tables using the wildcards or specifying the -t many times

- -T exclude the named table from the dump. It's possible to exclude multiple tables using the wildcards or specifying the -T many times

- -x do not dump the grant/revoke privileges

- –binary-upgrade is used only for the in place upgrade program pg_upgrade. Is not intended for general usage.

- –insert option dumps the data as INSERT command instead of the COPY. The restore with this option is very slow because each statement is parsed and executed individually.

- –column-inserts results in the data exported as INSERT commands with all the column names specified.

- –disable-dollar-quoting disables the dollar quoting for the function's body and uses the standard SQL quoting.

- –disable-triggers output the statements for disabling the triggers before the data load and the statements for enabling the triggers after the data load. This way the foreign keys will not fail during the data load. The switch have effect on plain text export only.

- –exclude-table-data=TABLE skips the data dump for the named table. It's possible to specify multiple tables using the wildcards or specifying the option many times.

- –no-security-labels doesn't include the security labels into the dump file

- –no-synchronized-snapshots allow to run a parallel export with PostgreSQL pre 9.2. However the database shall not change it's data until all of the dump workers are connected to the database.

- –no-tablespaces do not dump the statements setting the tablespace for the relations.

- –no-unlogged-table-data does not export data for the unlogged tables.

- –quote-all-identifiers cause all the identifiers to be enclosed in double quotes.

- –section option specifies one of the three export's sections. Applies only to plain text format.

  - pre-data contains the definitions for the tables, the views and the functions
  - data contains the table data
  - post-data contains the constraints definitions, the create index statements and the eventual GRANT REVOKE commands

- –serializable-deferrable uses a serializable transaction for the dump, to ensure the database state is consistent. The dump before starting waits for a point in the transaction stream without anomalies in order to avoid the risk of serialization_failure.

- –use-set-session-authorization sets the objects ownership using the command SET SESSION AUTHORIZATION instead of the ALTER OWNER. SET SESSION AUTHORIZATION requires the super user privileges whereas ALTER OWNER doesn't.

ATTENTION

When using the -n and -N switches pg_dump tries to resolve all dependencies. However something could be missing due to certain limitations. Therefore there's no guarantee the dump made with -n and -N can be successfully restored.

ATTENTION (Cont.) --

When both -n and -N are given, the behavior is to dump just the schema that matches at least one -n switch but no -N switches.

The switch –serializable-deferrable is not useful for the backup used only for disaster recovery and should be used only when the dump should be reloaded into a read only database which needs to get a consistent state compatible with the origin's database.

10.2   Performance tips

pg_dump is designed to have a minimal impact on the running cluster. However modifications for the backed up relations are blocked until the end of the backup. VACUUM during pg_dump is less effective because snapshot held by pg_dump prevents recycling of the dead rows generated during the backup.

10.2.1   Avoid remote backups

The pg_dump can connect to remote databases like any other PostgreSQL client. It seems reasonable to use the program installed on a centralized storage and use it to dump locally from the remote clusters. However even when using compressed format, the bandwidth can be saturated because compression is done as final step after the dump which always flows over the network uncompressed.

In order to speed up the dump over the network it is better to save locally the logical dump in custom or directory format and copy the dump contents with programs like rsync or scp.

10.2.2   Check for slow cpu cores

PostgreSQL is not multi threaded. Each backend is attached to just one cpu core. When pg_dump starts it opens a database backend which exports the database objects. The pg_dump process receives the data output from the backend saving in the chosen format. The single cpu's speed is then critical to avoid bottleneck. In order to improve the dump speed the parallel export can be used.

10.2.3   Check for the available locks

PostgreSQL uses the locks in order to enforce the schema and data consistency. For example, when a table is accessed for reading an access share lock is set to prevent the table's structure change. The locks on the relations are stored into the pg_locks table. This table is quite unique because has a limited amount of rows. The total available rows in pg_locks is determined with the formula:
max_locks_per_transaction * (max_connections + max_prepared_transactions)

However, if the database have complex schema with hundreds of relations, the backup can use all of the available slots and fail with an out of memory error. Changing the parameters max_locks_per_transaction,
max_connections, max_prepared_transactions requires restart.

10.3   pg_dump under the bonnet

The pg_dump source code gives a very good picture of what pg_dump does.

The first thing the process does is setting the correct transaction's isolation level. Each server's version requires a different isolation level.

Before the version 9.1 PostgreSQL implemented a soft SERIALIZABLE isolation which behaved more like the REPETABLE READ. Version 9.1 implemented a real SERIALIZABLE isolation level. The strictest isolation level SERIALIZABLE is used only when pg_dump is executed with the option – serializable-deferrable. The switch have effect only if the remote server is a version 9.1 or greater. The transaction is also set to READ ONLY when supported by the server, in order to limit the XID consumption.

Server version	Command
>= 9.1	REPEATABLE READ, READ ONLY
>= 9.1 with –serializable-deferrable	SERIALIZABLE, READ ONLY, DEFERRABLE
>= 7.4	SERIALIZABLE READ ONLY
<7.4	SERIALIZABLE

Table 10.1: pg_dump's transaction isolation levels

From version 9.3 pg_dump supports parallel dump using the snapshot exports seen in 5.11.2. As the snapshot export is supported from version 9.2 it is possible to dump in parallel using a newer pg_dump client from a PostgreSQL 9.2. However, if we want to dump in parallel from pre 9.2 versions it is possible to use the option –no-synchronized-snapshots which tells pg_dump to not execute a snapshot export. In this case, in order to have the data to be read consistently the database shouldn't accept write operations until all the export processes have connected to the server.

The parallel dump is possible only if used with directory format. The pg_restore program from version 9.3 can do a parallel restore using the directory format as source dump.

10.4   pg_dumpall

pg_dumpall does not have all the pg_dump's options. The program basically dumps all the cluster's databases in plain format.

However, pg_dumpall is very useful if we need to dump global objects like users and tablespaces. The switch –globals-only lets pg_dumpall to save the the global object definitions in plain text.

The following example shows the program's execution and the contents of the output file.

```
pg_dumpall --globals-only -f globals.sql
cat globals.sql

--
-- PostgreSQL database cluster dump
--

SET default_transaction_read_only = off;

SET client_encoding = 'UTF8';
SET standard_conforming_strings = on;

--
-- Roles
--

CREATE ROLE postgres;
ALTER ROLE postgres WITH SUPERUSER INHERIT CREATEROLE
    CREATEDB LOGIN REPLICATION BYPASSRLS;
CREATE ROLE usr_replica;
ALTER ROLE usr_replica WITH NOSUPERUSER INHERIT
    NOCREATEROLE NOCREATEDB LOGIN NOREPLICATION
    NOBYPASSRLS PASSWORD '
    md502093d3e9976e7a796b5be0dfa35d972';


--
-- Tablespaces
--

CREATE TABLESPACE ts_test OWNER postgres LOCATION '/
    home/postgres/data/11/tbs/ts_test';


--
-- PostgreSQL database cluster dump complete
```

EXAMPLE (Cont.)

--

Chapter 11

Restore

An ancient Italian proverb tells:

Il backup è quella cosa che andava fatta prima.

A rough translation could be something like this: **the backup is something to do before (the disaster strikes)**.
The concept of a backup is quite confusing. Some people wrongly believe that executing a local backup is sufficient to ensure the recover of the data.
In the real world a valid backup is present only if three conditions are true.

- The backup is taken

- The backup is copied on a separate machine

- The backups is used to test the restore periodically

In this chapter we'll take a look to the fastest and possibly the safest way to restore the saved dump along with an example of a periodical restore test setup.

As pg_dump can save in different formats the way we run the restore is determined by the dump format.

The simplest but yet the less flexible way is restoring from the plain format. The custom and the directory formats give the best performance in particular on multi processor systems.

We'll also look to the database configuration in order to improve performance of restore trading off temporarily the cluster's reliability.

11.1 The plain format

As seen in 10 the pg_dump's default output is plain SQL. The SQL script generated in this way gives no choice except loading it into the database using psql. The script is just a sequence of SQL statements written in the correct order for rebuilding the database structure and contents.

Despite the reduced flexibility this format has some advantages. For example it's possible to edit the statements using a text editor. However if the dump is big this operation can become difficult even when using editors that are capable of managing large text files.

If the backup strategy in plain text is to have the schema and the data in two separate files then the file with the data must be generated with pg_dump using the switch --disable-triggers, otherwise the foreign keys will prevent the data restore.

To better explain this concept we create a new database and a simple data structure within it. We have two tables one for storing the city name and another for the addresses. A foreign key is created between the tables to enforce the referential integrity.

```
db_test=# CREATE DATABASE db_addr;
CREATE DATABASE
db_test=# \c db_addr
You are now connected to database "db_addr" as user "
    postgres".
db_addr=# CREATE TABLE t_address
        (
                i_id_addr serial,
                i_id_city integer NOT NULL,
                t_addr text,
                CONSTRAINT pk_id_address PRIMARY KEY (
                    i_id_addr)
        )
;
CREATE TABLE
db_addr=# CREATE TABLE t_city
        (
                i_id_city       serial,
                v_city          character varying (255)
                    ,
                v_postcode      character varying (20),
                CONSTRAINT pk_i_id_city PRIMARY KEY (
                    i_id_city)
        )
;
CREATE TABLE
db_addr=# ALTER TABLE t_address ADD
            CONSTRAINT fk_t_city_i_id_city FOREIGN KEY
                (i_id_city)
            REFERENCES t_city(i_id_city)
              ON DELETE CASCADE
              ON UPDATE RESTRICT;
ALTER TABLE
```

Then we add some data to the tables.

```
INSERT INTO t_city
            (
              v_city,
              v_postcode
            )
        VALUES
            (
              'Leicester - Stoneygate',
              'LE2 2BH'
            )
        RETURNING i_id_city
;

 i_id_city
-----------
         3
(1 row)

db_addr=# INSERT INTO t_address
            (
              i_id_city,
              t_addr
            )
        VALUES
            (
              3,
              '4, malvern road '
            )
        RETURNING i_id_addr
;

 i_id_addr
-----------
         1
(1 row)
```

Now we run a pg_dump for the schema and another pg_dump for the data, saving the output in two different files. When saving the data only we don't use the switch the –disable-triggers.

EXAMPLE

```
pg_dump --schema-only db_addr > db_addr.schema.sql
pg_dump --data-only db_addr > db_addr.data.sql
```

The schema dump file contains all the DDL in the correct order for restoring the database structure .

The data dump file contains the COPY statements are generated in the correct order for having a restorable dump without the risk of referential integrity violation. This is possible because our example is very simple and there is only one correct dump order, where the table t_city is dumped before the table t_address. However in a real life scenario the referential order in the data only dump is not guaranteed. Therefore it's important to use the option –disable-trigger as safeguard from any possible risk of referential integrity violation.

If we generate the data only dump with –disable-trigger:

EXAMPLE

```
pg_dump --disable-triggers --data-only db_addr > db_addr.data.sql
```

We get the COPY statements enclosed between the disable and enable trigger statements.

EXAMPLE

```
ALTER TABLE t_address DISABLE TRIGGER ALL;

COPY t_address (i_id_addr, i_id_city, t_addr) FROM
    stdin;
1       3       4, malvern road
\.
```

169

```
ALTER TABLE t_address ENABLE TRIGGER ALL;
```

This way the triggers that enforce the foreign keys will not fire during the data restore ensuring that the data can be restored without caring about the dump order.

We can now create a new database to restore the dump.

EXAMPLE

```
db_test=# CREATE DATABASE db_addr_restore;
CREATE DATABASE
db_test=# \c db_addr_restore
You are now connected to database "db_addr_restore" as
    user "postgres".
db_addr_restore=# \i db_addr.schema.sql
SET
...
SET
CREATE EXTENSION
COMMENT
SET
SET
CREATE TABLE
ALTER TABLE
CREATE SEQUENCE
ALTER TABLE
ALTER SEQUENCE
CREATE TABLE
ALTER TABLE
CREATE SEQUENCE
ALTER TABLE
ALTER SEQUENCE
ALTER TABLE
...
ALTER TABLE
```

```
REVOKE
REVOKE
GRANT
GRANT
db_addr_restore=# \i db_addr.data.sql
SET
...
SET
ALTER TABLE
...
ALTER TABLE
 setval
--------
       1
(1 row)

 setval
--------
       3
(1 row)

db_addr_restore=# \d
                    List of relations
 Schema |            Name             |   Type   |  Owner
--
     -------+-----------------------------+----------+---------
 public | t_address                   | table    | postgres
 public | t_address_i_id_addr_seq     | sequence | postgres
 public | t_city                      | table    | postgres
 public | t_city_i_id_city_seq        | sequence | postgres
(4 rows)
```

11.2   The binary formats

The three binary formats supported by pg_dump are the custom, the directory
and the tar format. The first two support the selective access when restoring

and the parallel execution. These features make them the best choice for a flexible and reliable backup. From version 9.3 pg_restore supports parallel restore with both the custom and directory format. The tar format because of its limitations is a good choice only for saving small amount of data.

The custom format is a binary archive. It has a table of contents which can address the data saved inside the archive. The directory format is composed by toc.dat file where the schema is stored alongside with the references to the zip files where the tables contents are saved. For each table there is a gz mapped inside the toc. Each file contains command, COPY or insert, for reloading the data in the specific table.

The restore from the binary happens via the pg_restore program which has almost the same switches as pg_dump's as seen in 10.1. This is the pg_restore's help output.

EXAMPLE

```
pg_restore --help
pg_restore restores a PostgreSQL database from an archive created
    by pg_dump.

Usage:
  pg_restore [OPTION]... [FILE]

General options:
  -d, --dbname=NAME        connect to database name
  -f, --file=FILENAME      output file name
  -F, --format=c|d|t       backup file format (should be automatic)
  -l, --list               print summarized TOC of the archive
  -v, --verbose            verbose mode
  -V, --version            output version information, then exit
  -?, --help               show this help, then exit

Options controlling the restore:
  -a, --data-only          restore only the data, no schema
  -c, --clean              clean (drop) database objects before
```

```
        recreating
-C, --create                create the target database
-e, --exit-on-error         exit on error, default is to continue
-I, --index=NAME            restore named index
-j, --jobs=NUM              use this many parallel jobs to restore
-L, --use-list=FILENAME     use table of contents from this file
    for
                            selecting/ordering output
-n, --schema=NAME           restore only objects in this schema
-N, --exclude-schema=NAME   do not restore objects in this schema
-O, --no-owner              skip restoration of object ownership
-P, --function=NAME(args)   restore named function
-s, --schema-only           restore only the schema, no data
-S, --superuser=NAME        superuser user name to use for
    disabling triggers
-t, --table=NAME            restore named relation (table, view,
    etc.)
-T, --trigger=NAME          restore named trigger
-x, --no-privileges         skip restoration of access privileges
    (grant/revoke)
-1, --single-transaction    restore as a single transaction
--disable-triggers          disable triggers during data-only
    restore
--enable-row-security       enable row security
--if-exists                 use IF EXISTS when dropping objects
--no-comments               do not restore comments
--no-data-for-failed-tables do not restore data of tables that
    could not be
                            created
--no-publications           do not restore publications
--no-security-labels        do not restore security labels
--no-subscriptions          do not restore subscriptions
--no-tablespaces            do not restore tablespace assignments
--section=SECTION           restore named section (pre-data, data,
    or post-data)
--strict-names              require table and/or schema include
    patterns to
```

173

Most of the pg_restore options are the same as for pg_dump. This is the reason why the custom and the directory archive are the most flexible within the pg_dump's formats. After they are generated it is possible to chose what to restore and how using the same archive instead of dumping from the running database.

pg_restore requires at least a file to process and an optional database connection for performing the restore. If the connection is omitted then pg_restore's output is sent to the standard output. It's possible to specify a file for sending the output using the switch -f.

This option comes handy if we want to check and verify that the dump file can be read. In this case redirecting pg_restore's output to /dev/null and checking for the program's exit code will help us to detect issues with the archive.

It's possible to improve restore speed if we restore from a custom or directory

174

archive against a database connection on a multi core system. The switch -j allow us to specify how many parallel jobs we want to run during the data load and index creation.

The switch -C is used to create the target database before starting the restore. The connection needs also an alternate existing database to connect before the database listed in the archive is created. The simplest choice is to use template1 as temporary target database.

11.3   Restore performances

When disaster strikes the main goal is to get the database up and running as fast as possible. Loading the data is normally fast as the data is stored using the COPY command.

The real bottleneck is in the post-data section which operations, creating indices and constraints, requires CPU intensive operations with random disk access. In large databases restoring the post-data section can require up to 10 times the time necessary to restore the data section. Running the restore in parallel jobs can improve the operation's speed but sometimes this is not enough.

The postgresql.conf file can be tweaked in order to improve the restore at the cost of having a less reliable configuration. In case when database is already not operational, we can use the emergency configuration for the restore time, and afterwards replace it back by the production settings. What follows are the emergency configuration settings for having as fast as possible restore with pg_restore using a custom or directory archive.

11.3.1   shared_buffers

Bulk load operations may generate an high eviction rate from the shared buffer without taking advantage of the block caching. In this case we may reduce the size of the shared buffer as this will not affect the load speed. In doing so we'll make more memory available for per user processes when the post-data section is restored. However there is no fixed rule for resizing the shared buffer. A gross approximation could be to give at least 10 MB for each parallel job. The shared buffer size shouldn't be less than 512 MB though.

11.3.2   wal_level

The parameter wal_level sets the amount of redo records to store in the WAL segments. PostgreSQL sets the value to replica which is necessary when using the WAL archival for configuring standby servers or physical backups. Before starting the reload the wal_level should be set to minimal in order to reduce the WAL generation rate.

11.3.3   fsync

Turning off the fsync can improve the speed of restore. As having fsync turned off can result in data loss in case of power failure this setting should be changed only for the restore.

11.3.4   max_wal_size, checkpoint_timeout

The checkpoint is a periodic event in the database activity. When it occurs all the dirty pages in the shared buffer are flushed to their corresponding data files. This can interfere with the restore's bulk operations. The frequency of the checkpoints is controlled by max_wal_size and checkpoint_timeout. Increasing the value of max_wal_size to several GB, accordingly with the pg_wal size, and checkpoint timeout to the maximum value allowed, 1 day, will reduce the risk of having unnecessary IO caused by the frequent checkpoints.

11.3.5   autovacuum

Turning off the autovacuum will reduce the unnecessary IO avoiding the table's vacuum while restore is in progress.

11.3.6   max_connections

Reducing the max connections to the number of restore jobs plus an extra headroom of five connections will limit the memory consumption caused by the unused memory slots and will allow a better redistribution of the free memory on the system.

11.3.7   port and listen_addresses

When the database is restoring nobody except pg_restore and the DBA should access it. Changing the port to a different value and disabling the listen addresses except for the localhost is a quick and easy solution to avoid the normal users connecting to the database while it is being restored.

11.3.8   maintenance_work_memory

This parameter affects the creation speed of indices and constraints. Large amount of memory assigned to the backend will have the indices that fit in maintenance_work_memory to be built in memory with great speed improvement. The maintenance_work_memory's size should be set evaluating how much free RAM is available on the system. This value should be reduced by a 20% if the total available RAM is under 10 GB or 10% if the RAM installed is more than 10 GB. This reduction is necessary to leave some memory available for operating system and other processes.

After determining how much memory we should use for PostgreSQL we have to subtract the shared_buffer's size. Finally the rest of the memory should be divided between the number of max connections.

As example, if we have a system with the RAM size of 26 GB. If we configure the shared_buffer to be 2 GB and we set max_connections to 10, then the maintenance_work_mem size will be 2.14 GB.

EXAMPLE

```
26 - 10% = 23.4
23.4 - 2 = 21.4
21.4 / 10 = 2.14
```

Part IV

Appendix

Appendix A

Versioning and support policy

The PostgreSQL version number was composed by three integers up to the version 9.6. Since the version 10 the version numbering switched to two numbers only.

The first and second number up to the version 9.6 and the first number from the version 10 onward is the major version. Major version releases add internal changes that make data area not compatible between the major versions. A major release happens usually in the last quarter of the year, every year.

The last number is the minor version. Minor releases are scheduled each quarter and include bug fixes merged into the codebase. Upgrading a minor version usually requires just the binary upgrade and the cluster restart. However sometimes some extra actions are required. Version release notes report such information and additional steps to be taken.

The PostgreSQL project aims to fully support a major release for five years. The policy is applied on a best-effort basis.

Version	Supported	First release date	End of life date
11	Yes	October 2018	November 2023
10	Yes	October 2017	November 2022
9.6	Yes	September 2016	November 2021
9.5	Yes	January 2016	February 2021
9.4	Yes	December 2014	December 2019
9.3	No	September 2013	September 2018
9.2	No	September 2012	September 2017
9.1	No	September 2011	September 2016
9.0	No	September 2010	September 2015
8.4	No	July 2009	July 2014

Table A.1: End Of Life (EOL) dates

The complete list of versions is available at
https://www.postgresql.org/support/versioning/

Appendix B

A couple of things to know before start coding...

What follows is meant for developers approaching the PostgreSQL universe. PostgreSQL is more than a database. It's a fantastic infrastructure for building powerful applications. However in order to use it at its best there are some things to consider. Taking into account how PostgreSQL works it can make the difference between a magnificent success or a miserable failure.

B.1   SQL is your friend

Recently rise of the NOSQL engines has shown more than ever that the SQL language is alive and kicking. Anybody that wants to take the best from the data model should use SQL. Shortcuts like the ORMs sooner or later will show their limits. Despite its bad reputation the SQL language is very simple to understand. Since the beginning it has been designed to have few English keywords and a structured syntax which reflects the underlying database layer.

Mastering the SQL is slow and and not so simple process which requires some sort of empathy with the DBMS. Asking for advice from the database experts in house or on the Internet, when building a new design is always a good idea.

B.2 The design comes first

Forgetting that the data layer and the database are foundation of the application is bad. The rise of the ORM[1] has made this mistake happening more frequently.

The database design is a complex and important task that requires attention and shouldn't be delegated to an automated tool.
It doesn't matter if the database is simple or the project is small. Nobody knows how successful could be a new idea. A robust design will make the project scale properly.

B.3 Clean coding

Writing decently formatted code is something any developer should do. This have a couple of immediate advantages. Improves the code readability when other developers need to review it. Makes the code more manageable when, for example, is read months after it was written. Such good practice forgets constantly to include the SQL. It is quite common to find long queries written all lowercase on one line with keywords used as identifiers.

Trying to read such queries is a nightmare. Often it takes more time in reformatting the queries rather than doing performance tuning itself. The following guidelines are a good reference for writing decent SQL and avoid a massive headache to the DBA.

B.3.1 The identifier's name

Any DBMS has its way of managing the identifiers. PostgreSQL converts all lowercase. This doesn't work very well with the camel case. It's still possible to mix upper and lower case letters enclosing the identifier name between double quotes. But that means the quoting should be put everywhere. Using the underscores instead of the camel case is simpler.

---

[1] I dislike the ORMs

B.3.2   Self explaining schema

When a database structure becomes complex it is very difficult to say what is what and what are relations with other objects. A design diagram or a data dictionary can help. But they can be outdated or not available. Using a simple notation to add to the relation's name will give an immediate outlook of the object's kind.

Object	Prefix
Table	t_
View	v_
Btree Index	idx_bt_
GiST Index	idx_gst_
GIN Index	idx_gin_
Unique index	u_idx_
Primary key	pk_
Foreign key	fk_
Check	chk_
Unique key	uk_
Type	ty_
Sql function	fn_sql_
PlPgsql function	fn_plpg_
PlPython function	fn_plpy_
PlPerl function	fn_plpr_
Trigger	trg_
rule	rul_

A similar approach can be used for column names, making the data type immediately recognizable.

Type	Prefix
Character	c_
Character varying	v_
Integer	i_
Text	t_
Bytea	by_
Numeric	n_
Timestamp	ts_
Date	d_
Double precision	dp_
Hstore	hs_
Custom data type	ty_

B.3.3   Query formatting

Having a properly formatted query helps to understand which objects are involved in the request and their relations. Even a simple query can be difficult to understand if badly written.

EXAMPLE

```
select * from debitnoteshead a join debitnoteslines b
    on debnotid
where a.datnot=b. datnot and b.deblin >1;
```

Let's list the query's issues.

- using lowercase keywords makes it difficult to distinguish them from the identifiers

- the wildcard * mask which fields are really needed; returning all the fields consumes more bandwidth than required; it prevents the index only scans

- the meaningless aliases like a and b are confusing the query's logic

- without proper indention the query logic cannot be understood

Despite existence of tools capable to prettify such queries, their usage doesn't solve the root problem. Writing decently formatted SQL helps to create a mental map of what the query should do removing the confusion when building final SQL.

The following rules should be kept in mind constantly when writing SQL.

- All SQL keywords should be in upper case

- All the identifiers and keywords should be grouped at same indention level and separated with a line break

- In the SELECT list avoid the wildcard *

- Specify explicitly the join method in order to make it clear in the query's logic

- Adopt meaningful aliases

This is the prettified query.

EXAMPLE

```
SELECT
        productcode,
        noteid,
        datnot
FROM
        debitnoteshead head
        INNER JOIN
                debitnoteslines lines
                ON
                            head.debnotid=lines.
                                debnotid
                    AND     head.datnot=lines.
                        datnot
WHERE
                lines.deblin>1
    ;
```

The database administration is weird. It's very difficult to explain what a DBA does. It's a job where the statement "failure is not an option" is the rule Number Zero. A DBA usually works in antisocial hours, with a very tight time schedule.

Despite the strange reputation, a database expert is an incredible resource for building up efficient designs. Nowadays it is very simple to set up a PostgreSQL cluster. Even with the default configuration the system is so efficient that under normal load doesn't show any problems. This could look like a fantastic feature but actually is a really bad thing. Any mistake at design level is hidden and when the problem appears it might be too late to fix it.

This final advice is probably the most important of the entire chapter. If you have a DBA don't be shy. Ask for any suggestion, even if the solution seems obvious or if the design seems simple. The database layer is a universe full of pitfalls where a small mistake can result in a very big problem.

Of course if there's no DBA, that's bad. Never sail without a compass. Never start a database project without an expert's advice. Somebody to look after of the most important part of the business, the foundation.

Appendix C

Contacts

- Email: thedoctor@pgdba.org
- Twitter: @4thdoctor_scarf
- Blog: http://www.pgdba.org

List of Figures

List of Tables

Index